MORE THAN LILIES

ERIN KENNEDY

DEDICATION

I am dedicating this book first and foremost to God. I would not be where I am, or who I am without Him.

I also would like to dedicate this book to my parents and sister, Michael, Lisa, and Marissa. Thank you for always believing in me, you make my world go round.

2 Corinthians 12:9

But he said to me, "My grace is sufficient for you, for my power is made perfect in weakness." Therefore, I will boast all the more about my weaknesses, so that Christ's power may rest on me.

TABLE OF CONTENTS

PROLOGUE

More than Lilies, a phrase warranted from Matthew 6, and a phrase that carries significant weight in my heart. More than lilies means that although flowers quickly go through their cycles, God still clothes them with beauty and splendor. God still cares about the minute details. He pursues our hearts and desires to be known by us. So where is the disconnect? Why is that not evident in the religion we practice? Why is there a God of the universe that cares so deeply and people who are aware of it, but fail to get that message across? Why does the church send people running? These are all questions that have crossed my mind. This is why I am writing - to recognize the common practices that often send people further away from the Father rather than drawing them into His open arms. I want to see the lost, found; the hurting, healed; and the broken, whole. I want to see less and less people with bitterness towards Christ due to the actions of those who follow Him. I hope that some of the stereotypes begin to be negated by a movement of love and authenticity like never before.

This all roots from my experiences and the times that I have experienced hurt from those I least expected. As for some back story, I am currently a college student living in New Jersey, USA. I have known Christ for some time now and have a heart for missions and serving others. I am beyond excited for the future ahead of me and look forward to what God has in store. In 2022, I went on a trip to Northeast Georgia, where I expected to pour out and serve others. Little did I know, this trip would be one of receiving just as much as it was giving. I received healing, freedom, and joy; and in turn, I got to pour out those beautiful attributes as well. I am planning on going into missions wherever the Lord calls me. As I have known this for some time, I do want you to know that 100% of the proceeds will be going towards my missionary endeavors.

God has laid writing this book on my heart, and I cannot wait to see the healing it brings me as I walk through this journey of putting what I have learned into words. I am expectant and pray that what the Lord has done in my life will bring healing and freedom through this book. As you read, I challenge you to not take what I say as truth. I challenge you to question, to test it against the Word of God, and to be open towards what He may have for you. More than anything, I pray that this book will only be a small part of the story God has written for you. I am grateful for this opportunity and look forward to filling the pages to come.

CHAPTER 1

CHURCH PEOPLE

Before you put the book down because you are a church person and think you are about to get judged or condemned, know that I too am a church person. I am a church person who grew up around church people. Where are you going with this, you may ask. Well, I guess I will get right into it. To preface, I will not be naming any churches, denominations, or people groups, and you will come to know why.

I WANT TO CHANGE

I was a young girl attending a small Christian school. I grew up there, played sports there, and learned about God there. I had friends who walked through life with me and teachers who saw me grow as the years went on. In the early years, it was what some would call an oasis. I came to know about God in so many ways.

I loved knowing the school property like the back of my hand it truly was an extension of my home. I have so many fond memories of the time spent there and of the people that were a part of my life because of my attendance at the school.

Around the age of seven or eight, I asked Jesus into my heart. I do not remember the date, or even the time of year. All I remember is stepping into my bright pink room with violently purple shag carpet, and a loft bed. I remember getting on my knees and praying for Jesus to save me, to forgive me of my sins, and that I wanted to do life with Him. Little did I know the journey He had ahead of me. I believe to this day that I will always have a part of me that feels just like when I first got saved. A young girl with a childlike wonder of all that God can do in my life.

As a young child, I stepped into the spotlight. I was strong academically and athletically, and I had an even stronger determination. I was determined to try everything and excel at everything. When it came to most things, I was simply good at them. In all honesty, school came naturally, and so did sports. I quickly became the girl that was good at things. Yes, I feel like it may come across wrong, but it is my story. Teachers loved me, and my parents did not think twice about what I did, solely because they knew I would be harder on myself than they were on me. That. That is where the self-hate began. I was the golden child when it came to sports and school, but I hated who I was as a person. I was loud, demanding, and bossy. I was not me. I knew that for a fact, but when you grow up with people who know your parents and took care of you as a child, change does not come easy. In all honesty, for me it may have been impossible. I came to a point where I was so disgusted by who I was that I truly craved change, but I did not know how to get there.

Imagine this. A seventh-grade girl, walking outside with her best friend on a warm Jersey spring day. She walked beside the only friend she ever felt saw her as who she really was. In that moment, she thought about herself inwardly and who she was outwardly, and the words bled through her lips "I want to change". However, in reality she was crying out, this isn't me. I love people, and care for them, I do not want to ever be perceived as mean. All I want is to be seen for the true me. The me that God sees. The me that God saved. I want to change into who I innately am.

For the life of me, I cannot remember what my friend replied, all I remember is the true brokenness and helplessness that I felt. I remember her acknowledging my heart, but I don't think she knew the depth of my longing to change. She just knew me, and still loved me despite my outer personality. Thankfully I know now that God is in the redemption business, and my story did not end there.

CHRISTIANESE

This is the hard part. However, I have decided to be honest as I step into sharing my view of church people. First and foremost, I hate generalizations. I am a part of a generation that has been stereotyped and generalized more than any before it. It is disgusting. So when I speak of church people, I by no means mean every single church person out there. I am a church person, I love church people, and some of my closest friends and mentors are church people. Yet, like any other group in the world, we need to work on ourselves and every once in a while, we need a reality check. So here it is:

Matthew 22: 38-39

This is the first and greatest commandment. And a second is like it: 'Love your neighbor as yourself.'

It may seem off that I share the second commandment that Jesus brings to the table. Yet, I feel that most people understand the first, to love God with all their heart. Despite outward actions and judgments, I believe most church people do love God, but are human. This means we struggle with the second commandment as our daily lives are intertwined with each other's. I grew up with hate being bred into my heart without me even realizing it, in the place the love of God should abound, the church. I was told not to accept certain denominations, walks of life, or people who disagreed with my core values. I was trained to recognize differences. This is heartbreaking because it is not just a part of my story. It is a part of modern-day Christianity as a whole. The church has aimed to feed into inclusivity at the cost of widespread division. We are so caught up in our grievances with each other, we do not recognize the broken world we are called to love.

Aside from that, let me take you on a little thought process of mine.

Imagine you are living in the worst conditions you personally can think of. You are hungry, tired, and will do anything you can in your power to get water and some sustenance in your body. You have been beaten brutally by people you trusted because you have fallen out of their social standing. You have nothing to give, so you lay down in the middle of town, and pray for the endless sleep that is rounding the corner to come quicker. You then are grabbed violently and tossed across the road. You are suddenly a spectacle in a crowd of people. People who were once your friends. Then as your former coworker approaches and looks dead into your eyes that are begging for the slightest bit of mercy, they spit in your face. At this moment, no one in their right mind would help you. It would mean certain death, certain destruction for you both.

Now imagine you are on the other side. You are a member of the crowd. You used to go to church with this woman, she used to watch your kids when you were sick. What do you do? Do you even have a chance standing up for her? If so, how and when? She is nearing death as you ponder your thoughts. Do you help her?

That is a question you and only you can answer. I have sat with the Lord and played out situations like these. I think I know what I would do, but in reality I have no clue.

The sad truth that I am getting at is church people are typically the ones spitting. There is a stigma of judgment that encompasses the western church. A stigma that is not completely invalidated. There are so many who have forgotten what it means to love. We yell Jesus, but choose to forget how He lived His life. He served the least of these. He chose the lower class to be His disciples and closest friends. He ate with tax collectors who most would not even glance at. He stepped in and saved women who had filthy pasts. He healed those society believed earned their disabilities. He was counter cultural. Nevertheless, we find ourselves stuck in a rut of religion to the point that we cannot see past our own preconceived notions to love the very ones Jesus died for.

Let's walk through another situation.

You walk into a church service. Next to you is a stranger you have never seen in church before. You notice a rainbow flag tattoo on their ankle, something so small, but something that invites you into the story of who they are. Worship ends, one of the elders goes over the announcements, and exciting events that are coming up. From the corner of your eye, you can tell the stranger is hanging onto every word being said. The stranger is searching. The message begins, and it is good, and you find yourself listening intently, but also praying for this soul next to you. Then about fifteen minutes into the message, a quick joke is mentioned demeaning the LGBTQ+ community. So subtle and naturally inserted into the message, and from that there are muffled laughs from the congregation. In this very moment, your heart drops as the stranger's eyes next to you glaze over. Checked out. Just like that. To your surprise the stranger does not leave. The message ends, and the stranger slips out the back never to be seen again.

This is a situation similar to ones I have witnessed myself. It is so disheartening. So in my life, I have decided that I never want to be fluent in Christianese. Considering that I grew up going to a private school, it was my first language. I knew a lot about God, and I knew a lot about what God said was wrong. I voiced that too. What I did not realize was in my moments of spewing Christianese at people, I was estranging them from the love of Christ. I was helping them build walls, because in reality who would want to be a part of something so hateful. Situations, like the aforementioned, exploit our deficit of love within the Christian community.

I often think of how embarrassing and condescending it is when someone speaks over my head in my professional settings. I find it incredibly humiliating. I am currently interning at an engineering consulting company. At first, everything went over my head, I was confused and lost. Over time, I learned the lingo, but in all honesty, the first month and a half was hard. However, I was thinking about the early days now that I love where I am at; and I realized that these people were not doing it intentionally. They just know their occupation well. That is how some Christians come across and most times it is not intentional. Yet, new believers or people who are hearing about God for the first time may feel humiliated or embarrassed if we are not aware of our words. This also aids in people putting up walls, because no one likes to be humiliated and often people avoid situations or topics in order to avoid further humiliation.

That being said, I am one to joke around, but God has convicted me by showing me situations like the one above. He has illuminated the fact that our words carry an infinite amount of weight. Weight that can burden someone for years. The relief is that we have a God that is willing to carry our burdens, but a lot of people do not know that, or have been hurt and do not want to open up to the God whose followers are the ones who caused them to bear the burden.

Yet again, it's okay, because our God is a Redeemer who can redeem people who have been hurt as well as those who have caused it.

JUDGMENT

Judgment is defined by most as a determination sourced from a series of inquiries or more simply put, a thought out decision. In our world today, people so quickly think of judgment as what Christians do. In contrast, judgment is not always a bad thing. Judgment is, in the court of law, a well thought out decision that took time to be determined. Judgment in and of itself is intended to be thought out. Yet like most things, our modern culture has twisted judgment into something that is instantaneous. What most describe as a snap judgment.

As the recipient and perpetrator, I have come to know different aspects of judgment. I grew up being the perpetrator. As I said before, I was brought up to know a lot about what God did not like, from being in a Christian school. In retrospect, I saw a lot of the love of Christ there too, but I think as a kid the former stood out more. Now I just see people who were fallible doing their best to raise up the next generation of followers of Christ. Anyway, (don't mind the first of many bunny trails) I knew what God did not like. I noticed more and more how easy it was to think poorly of someone within the first five seconds of meeting them. This is the downfall of our society. In reality, it is laced through every person to some degree. I know it is, I have seen it in all different walks of life, and in different seasons of my own. More than anything, I have come to recognize this, but not to be surprised by it. Why? Because a person on their own is weak, but those who walk together are not easily conquered. This is why the enemy plays the division card more than any other of his old deck.

Ecclesiastes 4:12

Though one may be overpowered, two can defend themselves. A cord of three strands is not quickly broken.

As I have gotten older, I have experienced more of the recipient side of judgment. There is one attribute in my life that causes me to be a recipient of judgment. That I am a female, more specifically a female pursuing an engineering degree. I knew walking into this that I would be judged.

"It's a man's field"

"You're too young"

"You don't know what you actually want"

"You could do anything else"

"Women aren't meant for this"

All things I have heard, some intended maliciously and some purely intended, but still not okay. This has opened my eyes to the world of judgment. It has also humbled me because, God called me to it, but I could do something else. This realization has shaken me to the core as I recognize that a majority of the time, we judge people on something they cannot change. How heartbreaking?! That has made me rethink the severity of the fact that people are so much more than their body, face, or what they want to do in life.

For what life I have lived, I would say a key to life is becoming aware of your judgmental side. Notice I did not say to never judge. By no means is judging acceptable or justifiable, but we are human and becoming aware of your judgments, especially those that are instinctual, is the first step towards fixing the true problem.

REAL

Stemming from my realization of how hurtful judging can be, I have found infinite value in being real. Authenticity is something I craved as a child. As I mentioned, all I wanted was to change, and to let others see my authentic self.

I realized how much judgment littered my soul with ugliness, and how self-hatred bred discontentment in my life. This led to the idea of cultivating authenticity in my life. Later in my story, I will share the opportunity that God gave me to start over. That opportunity was truly when I was able to be my authentic self. However, I will share now what authenticity can bring into your life, and into others as well.

When I finally let go of the calloused, bossy side of myself, I felt a weight come off. The weight that I had self-imposed was my own expectations. Along with my thoughts, I also overestimated everyone else's expectations for me. I look back and chuckle, because in reality, they would have loved me no matter what and I was more in my head than anything. I came to recognize the fact that I would speak, but not live by: all that matters is what God thinks of me. It is the truth, and I think most followers of Christ can acknowledge that, but few live by it.

Stepping back for a minute, I want to touch on what acknowledging, but not living this truth can do to a soul. I speak from experience that it will just breed people pleasing tendencies. You start to crave the approval of others, even if you do not realize it. You want to be loved, and it may be for all the right reasons, but no one is loved by everyone. In fact, it says in the Word that people will hate you because they hate Christ. At some point, everyone comes to the conclusion that not everyone will like them. I promise you, the sooner the better. It frees your soul to live for the One. It frees your heart from the disappointment when someone does not like you. Lastly, it frees your schedule to serve Him instead of trying to gain the love of others.

Matthew 10:22

All men will hate you because of me, but he who stands firm to the end will be saved.

So live by the truth that His opinion is the only one that matters, but like most worthwhile attributes it will take practice, and that is okay.

I am still walking in this journey. The wildest part is when I start to feel confident, I catch myself pleasing people, or overanalyzing myself again. Some would say I am on an uphill journey with this specific area of my life. Rather than an uphill, I see it as a journey through a mountain range. There are hills, there are valleys, there are peaks, and there are divots. None less important than the prior. I find this important because there seems to be a stereotype of journeys and like I said, I hate stereotypes. It seems like people want to see you improve, but as soon as you digress even slightly, you have backslidden or failed. Yet, I have started to learn to find beauty in the moments of weakness. More and more I have found His power comes to life in my everyday walk through my weakness. I have come to terms (somewhat- well it's a work in progress) with failure. God has challenged me in this area, and I am grateful for it because I have come to notice that He shows up and shows out when I fail. I see Him work in my failures which has caused me to recognize His hand in my successes. So if you are on a journey with some aspect of your life, chugging along as God helps you through, keep going. If you have fallen behind, it is okay, keep going. If you have come to a dead stop, keep going. I promise in the long run, you will never be perfect, but every single effort you put in will be worth the outcome. There is no such thing as a perfect journey, or a solely upward battle so walk with Him and cling to Him at all times, that is all that matters.

2 Corinthians 12:9

But he said to me, "My grace is sufficient for you, for my power is made perfect in weakness." Therefore, I will boast all the more about my weaknesses, so that Christ's power may rest on me.

WHAT CAN WE DO

So what can church people do? What should we pray into, what should we work on? Simply put: Love. Yet, the reality is that it doesn't always come that easy. My encouragement that has completely changed my walk is really digging into the life of Jesus in the Gospel.

Take time to note who He served, who He spent His time here on earth with. Even more so, take note of His actions. If we are, as a church body, aiming to be more like Christ, we need to invest more time knowing who He was.

CHAPTER 2

CROSSROADS

MY STORY

I title this part 'My Story', but in reality, this is just a turning point in my life, or a crossroad. I learned a lot in this season of life and have come to love sharing this part of my testimony.

Eighth grade Erin was the girl who wanted to change. Yet, little did I know that God saw that desire and had major plans in store for me. I was about to go on a winter retreat with my youth group when my mom told me I needed to start considering other schools instead of where I was at for high school. This thought had never occurred to me before, as the plan all along was to go to my private school until I graduated high school. That being said, I went into the retreat with my head spinning. I came out of the retreat with what I thought was a solution. I had decided to go to a public school a few towns over, where all my youth group friends attended. I told my mom and was set, but then there were factors that blatantly made it obvious that it was not the school for me. So there went solution number one. The next solution came from my mom: technical school. This idea was great except for two issues, I did not know what field I wanted to go into, and we missed enrollment. So at this time, I resorted to going back to my private school.

What about your own district's public school? Well, that was out of the question, I mean not even on the table from the very beginning. I was dead set against it and knew that out of all the options that was not even remotely on the horizon. So I settled into the idea of going back to my private school. I was not overly thrilled, but it was my comfort zone so I was fine with it.

Then came summer camp, a week I will never forget, a time that humbled me, challenged me, and in reality changed the course of my life. Sounds drastic, I know, but stick with me. The irony is the fact that this summer camp did not change the course of my life until after the trip.

It was August and ever since I was little, I have been a journal type of girl. I write everything down, quite literally, everything. This was also true when it came to summer camp. So here I was a month later reading back through the notes from summer camp when God spoke to me. The first major topic was legalism, which is the reason I was looking to leave my private school. Then it talked about faith. This was a subject that bled into the last: fear. I was petrified to go to my district's public school. I was not going to until this moment. I sat there amazed that God outlined what was going on in my life, in my own handwriting, without me realizing it. Then in my patio chair, I felt a rush of peace, the peace that passes all understanding. I knew the answer, I was going to my town's public school.

Philippians 4:7

And the peace of God, which transcends all understanding, will guard your hearts and your minds in Christ Jesus.

Over time, this was affirmed as my two closest friends also transferred with me. Later on, I will go more in depth of how this all played out in my life, but just know that it was better than anything I could have ever planned.

LEGALISM

There is a reason Christians are stereotyped the way they are. Some stereotypes are passed down from generation to generation with no true basis for them, but some are exaggerated around a small fact that is true. The latter is where I believe Christianity falls. The truth? People are imperfect, including Christians. Christians will let you down. Christians will hurt you. Christians will judge you. Christians will curse. Christians will fail. I can promise you that. The validity of those statements rings true. There is an innumerable amount of disappointment, hurt, and ill will caused by Christians. I am not going to justify it. I am not going to explain on behalf of every person. I am going to explain my experience in hopes that it sheds light on your experiences.

I have been there, I have walked into the group of Christians who are supposed to be loving and reflections of Jesus, but left feeling degraded, dismissed, and judged. The reality is I have been the perpetrator as well. It is the smiles that are forced, the pleasantries that are far from genuine, and the condescending 'better than you' comments. It is revolting. It is heartbreaking. The expectations and judgments that exude from these people can and will influence your view of God. Strongly. We lose sight of the Bible and what God wants because we start to aim to please the people who claim to be living out the Word of God, but make it nearly impossible to feel remotely close to the God who saved your soul.

This, this is legalism as I have encountered it. There are expectations: do not show your shoulders, do not speak up against those older than you, even if they are wrong, you are being watched, and will be called out when you slip up. It is toxic, it is consuming, and it is the furthest thing from what God has for you. There are all these walls put between you and the Father. Walls like wearing the right thing, saying the right thing, and acting the right way always. There are Christians that have pure intentions, but prioritize these small things over showing the love of Christ. It creates a false reality that there are Christians that have it all together. Even more so, the hearts of these Christians typically intend to spread the Word, but their actions and judgments actually send people further away.

The irony to me is that this is not a new issue. In the New Testament, Jesus encounters the 'religious leaders' on numerous accounts. He calls them out for their showy prayer and giving, and tells us that this is not what it is about. Rather it is about being genuinely surrendered and giving what you have no matter the worldly value. He challenges us to be like the woman with the singular coin rather than the rich who only gave to show off their 'righteousness'.

Mark 12:41-44

Jesus sat down opposite the place where the offerings were put and watched the crowd putting their money into the temple treasury. Many rich people threw in large amounts. But a poor widow came and put in two very small copper coins, worth only a fraction of a penny. Calling his disciples to him, Jesus said, "I tell you the truth, this poor widow has put more into the treasury than all the others. They all gave out of their wealth; but she, out of her poverty, put in everythingall she had to live on."

This is such a beautiful example of a heart matter. There is something surreal, even ethereal about a faith without rules, a faith that challenges the ordinary. This is what Christ calls us to, not a life of rules to be meticulously followed. I think that the undertones even beg the question of does the action matter or the intent of the heart. Both people acted in the same manner, they gave money, but Jesus commends the poor widow. Why? Because her heart was pure. Yet, some may have dismissed her for her lowly status. All based on judgment.

Fortunately, there is forgiveness in store for all. There is forgiveness for those who have sinned, which includes those that warp God's Word in such a way to condemn others. As well as anyone who has sinned in any way. Again, we serve a God who redeems. So although it breaks my heart when people are sent further from God due to legalism and judgments, I know He is still in the works in their life. I know that no one can rip those He loves from His hands, and that He will ultimately work everything for His good.

For instance, I have seen the religious side of Christianity, and noticed how it can be a massive turn off for those searching for God. But in that, I have learned how to be more of a reflection of Christ, because when it comes down to it, Christ had dinner with sinners, befriended tax collectors, and spent His days with prostitutes. I aspire to be as genuine as Christ, and I pray for those that have not found the relationship side of religion and the freedom that Christ's sacrifice brings. I pray that they begin to see Jesus as He was. He was countercultural, He was loving, He challenged others to love despite history.

He was the least religious person that truly longed for genuine relationships with people that were highly regarded, as well as those who were not acknowledged at all.

He never intended for His followers to condemn, but rather to love, to step to the world's level. Not to stay there, but to bring people to Him.

Christ called His disciples to be fishers of men. He called them in a way they understood. The analogy is beautiful. The men at that time would fish from a boat and in many instances Jesus spent time on the boat with them. From stories, we learn that they caught fish by throwing nets out. They did this while on the boat, not on the shore. They had to go into the water to find the fish. Just as they had to step onto the boat to be able to go find the fish in order to be effective, we as Christians are called to step into the world in order to be able to be fishers of men. Anyone that has fished in any manner knows you need to be close to their habitat to catch a fish. It is common sense. You are not going to catch a fish standing inland.

Yet, we live that out as Christians, and especially as legalists. We stand fifteen miles inland trying to catch fish. We stay in our churches with our crowds, and our comforts, and our judgments, and wonder why God's Word is not advancing in our areas. We are not going out, and if we do, we are yelling from the shore which everyone knows scares the fish away.

There needs to be initiative, just like fishermen often go out at different times of the day. The world is not going to come to us, we must go to them.

FAITH

Faith is a conundrum. Every ounce of our human flesh defies us having faith. We are wired to want to be independent, figure out things on our own, and in most cases, live in severe pridefulness. Faith calls us to be countercultural. It begs us to take the control we crave and leave it at the foot of the cross. We are called to live in opposition to what our flesh desires. Christ alone is what this world needs, but few are willing to live as a sacrifice.

Romans 12:1

Therefore, I urge you, brothers, in view of God's mercy, to offer your bodies as living sacrifices, holy and pleasing to Godthis is your spiritual act of worship.

As a young girl, I craved to be authentic and change from who I was to who I knew I was made to be. Yet, I sat with this opportunity of a lifetime to start over. An answered prayer was laid at my feet, but even then, I was afraid. I was nervous, and I did not know if I could do it.

"But God". One of my favorite phrases in the Bible. It challenges, it pleads for perseverance, and it shows that there is more. This part of my story was one of the most prominent "but God" moments. He challenged me to take the step of faith despite what I thought was possible or impossible. He just asked for obedience. He asked for a mustard seed, and that's all I had.

There is beauty in the unseen. Like I said above, faith that is unshaken is simply beautiful. It is something the world will never understand, because it typically defines what the world deems impossible. Yet, that makes it all the more fun. The thought of serving a God who does not know the word impossible is exhilarating, but also terrifying. He has no bounds, but we do. Our bounds limit us to be weary of His capabilities. Faith is what bridges the gap between our bounds and His plans for our life. Faith is the essential component that gives us the opportunity to live out the life He has in store for us. A wonderfully abundant life.

FEAR

Where to start, fear is crippling and can be seen in many manners. At the time, fear for me was embodied in my district's public school. I was terrified of the unknown. I did not know many people, I did not know the building, or the rooms. In fact on my first day, I got lost going to my first class. There was so much that I did not know, and that was foreign to me. The school I went to growing up was an extension of my family. I knew everyone and their mom, literally. I also knew that school like the back of my hand, I am pretty sure I had been in every room that was there.

The fear of facing thousands of new faces when I was used to having only a couple hundred was intimidating. Yet, this was a major life skill that I was going to have to learn sooner or later. I faced the first major change in my life, and it was incredibly hard. Many who know my testimony, know that I cried for the first few months of my new school, sometimes multiple times a week. I struggled a lot. I knew down to my core, for the first time that I genuinely could not do it. I had the loosest grip on my life that I had ever had at that point. I was broken down, but this right here, in the very face of fear, led to the largest crossroads in my life yet. I knew God. I knew all about Him. I had chapters of the Bible memorized word for word, I knew all the answers to the typical Christian questions. I knew what I knew. That being said, I also knew what to say and when to say it to portray myself as a perfect little Christian. To clarify, I am not saying that all of it was ingenuine, but I had way more head knowledge than heart knowledge at the time. As I mentioned, I came to know Jesus and God personally around eight years old, but freshman year of high school is when I came to need God, desperately and more apparently than ever before.

I came to know God in my heart more than I ever had before. I realized that the in between is where growth is inevitable. Growth is imperative, but it is uncomfortable. I came to know God intimately as He became very familiar with my tears. I knew that God had a plan, but I could not see where He was heading. I found an intimate relationship with God that was unlike anything else I had ever known. If it was not for the extreme discomfort, I would have never grown in my walk with the Lord in that capacity. This is when I truly recognized that all I need is Him, and I came to know that to my very core. Prior to this, I had the knowledge, I had the friends, I had the gifts of athleticism and intelligence. I had a privileged and protected life up until this point. I still was privileged, I just struggled more than I ever had. I remember vividly the sequence of the beginning of freshman year. In late July, I was still training with my private school for soccer. At the first official practice with the coaches, I rolled my ankle during warm up, but not a typical roll, more like a snap, crackle, pop kind of roll. I was stubborn and wanted to show out, so I ran through the rest of the practice. At the end, I got in the car and I remember pulling my sock off to a very large and blue ankle. That night I went to the hospital and was told that I sprained my ankle worse than most breaks. This was not a big deal until I came to the decision of switching schools about a week and a half into August. If I was going to transfer, I wanted to be on the soccer team. To my own fault, I persuaded the doctor that my ankle was healed when it was not and tried out for the team. I was nervous, and I think my relationship with sports fundamentally changed at this point. I equated sports with the me I used to hate. This then caused me to not try as much, in order to not become the 'star' and in essence the obnoxious person I used to be.

Yet, I also know it was God's provision when I did not make the soccer team. I did have one friend who was on the team, and I remember her asking me if I made it, and I told her no, but I was so at peace with it. Again, just basking in that peace that passes all understanding. This is when I would have expected myself to break down, but it was not.

Then about a month into school, I found myself on the roof outside of my room. Now it is a balcony, but before that it was just a roof that I frequented as a kid. I found myself in fetal position, weeping. I was overwhelmed. I had a heightened sense of my inability to do this on my own. I knew that I was in over my head, but more than anything I knew this was exactly where God wanted me. I knew that I was in that season of sheer loneliness, fear, and discomfort for a reason. A little while and a lot of tears later, my mom came out on my roof and found me. I cannot imagine her heart, finding her daughter uncontrollably crying on a roof, but she sat with me. She told me everything was going to be okay, and that I could go back to my private school. She told me I could choose either way, but she hated seeing me in so much distress. She told me no one would think of me any differently if I went back to my private school.

Then, in that moment, God spoke to me through my own words. This moment is one that I will cherish forever and was a defining time in my walk with Christ. I replied to all my mother's advice with a simple sentence. Moreover, one that has shaped my life and gotten me through many trials and tribulations. I said, "Just because it is hard does not mean it is not His will".

A lot of people ask what is one piece of advice you would give. That, right there, will always be my one piece of advice.

WHAT CAN WE DO

So what can we do as Christians to honor God in our crossroads? Approach them with an open heart. Crossroads are not easy, and God does not see them as something that we need to deal with on our own. Instead of pain, we should look at them as opportunities for growth. Also, we can look at them as opportunities to invite in community and bear each other's burdens. This is how we are meant to approach them. I think there is another reality that also should be acknowledged which is transparency. I cannot tell how different my childhood would have been if Christians in my life showed that they were not always okay. It seems taboo to let people know that you are going through difficult times, but we all are at one point or another and allowing others to see into that gives them the perception that Christians do not have it all together, and that is something I believe could truly change the dynamic between Christians and the world.

CHAPTER 3

YOUR CALLING

MY STORY

I have chosen to start this chapter with another part of my story because in reality that is all I can do. I cannot be God's voice in your life. I pray that He works through my words, but that will be His work and His work alone. I can only share what He has done in my life.

What is your calling? A daunting question to say the least. People seem to roam the earth searching for the answer, searching for their calling, purpose, and meaning. I was one of those people.

After I adjusted to high school, I came to love it. There was a beauty in that aspect of my life. At the same time, there was the side of my life that was heavily involved in church. I loved going, I loved serving, and I was there more than I think I realized at the time. As a kid, I grew up watching missions' teams leave each year for our church's trip to Mexico. I was mesmerized by the idea. I also had an aunt and uncle who served as missionaries in Africa, and I dreamed of the day I would get to go somewhere and 'do missions'. In order to go to Mexico, my church had an age requirement of thirteen. So you know, eighth grade summer, I was set. I was finally old enough and I was going to make it happen one way or the other. Then for the first time in years, the trip got canceled, I do not remember why, I just remember being devastated.

I now believe that it was because I was not ready. After a year in time, and a slew of experiences that radically deepened my walk with Christ had passed, it was time for the Mexico trip once again. I was ready and my heart was more in a place of service than it was a year prior. I signed up, fundraised, and went. Let me tell you my world view changed. I saw devastation like I had never before. I also saw genuine contentment like I had never before. My heart was moved.

Nevertheless, the real pivotal moment came the following year. Another year went by, and more growth, and another Mexico trip. This time was different. I knew what to expect, and even more so I longed to be there to serve.

Halfway through our two-week trip, we took a trip to a ranch. We brought all of the church we were serving and enjoyed a day of fellowship and fun on the Sabbath. It was beautiful, we hiked up a mountain, there was a pool, and people were being baptized. To say the least it was a joyful day. Then we all got back into the twelve passenger vans to drive back to the ministry where we were staying. This is when everything changed. I was in this white van with my teammates and Mexican friends, everyone was tired, but in a happy state of mind. In this moment, I should have been elated, rather I found myself heartbroken. I was crying. Fortunately, it was dark so no one realized. It was not a sob, or tears of joy. In fact, the only way I can describe it is like when you take something from a toddler, and the slow tears roll down their face.

Why was I crying? I was heartbroken that our time there was already halfway over. I was heartbroken that I had to go back to my normal privileged life and that I would fall back into American monotony. I did not want to. Every fiber of my being wanted to stay in Mexico. I was wrestling with God about it. That is why I was crying. That is when He revealed my calling to me. In the midst of a twelve passenger van on a road somewhere in the middle of Mexico, God whispered to my heart that I did not have to fall back into monotony, and that I could serve full time. In fact, that was what I was made to do.

Obviously, I was a sophomore in high school, and I did need to leave Mexico at the end of that week, but God was not talking about 2018. He was talking about life.

DISCERNING HIS VOICE

That specific part of my story will always be close to my heart, but I am well aware that not every aspect of God's will is so explicitly provided. I have seen God work in that way, a whisper on a bus or a word of direction through notes on my back patio. Yet, God also works and speaks in other ways as well. He does not always give us a direct answer.

This makes some decisions very hard, and over the years, when praying and asking for advice on decisions, I have often gotten one of two answers.

The first being, just pray about it. Prayer is essential, no doubt, but I have found a few issues with this piece of advice. Mainly, to be able to pray about something is a privilege. It should never be demeaned into something that is a last resort. It should be a first reaction, and should be fruitful. As I said, I am one for prayer, but oftentimes people use the 'just pray about it' method as a way to cop out of having to step out in faith. It becomes a waiting game that never ends, or brings you to the deadline of the decision with no clarity. This is not what God intends. God intends for us to have clarity, He intends to be in communication with us. He intends for us to be able to make decisions, or else He would not have given us free will. As well, the 'just pray about it' piece of advice can often come across as a dismissive answer. This can often be disheartening to the person asking. In my experience, when I have asked for advice and gotten this quick response, it left me feeling like the other person was brushing off my request. This has helped me see the other side of when people come to me. We are called to be in community and carry each other's burdens. That means that we are called to walk through life together, not just leave the person to try and pray through their own. In the very least, I would challenge you to pray with the person, if you have no advice to give. Another way to look at this is from the perspective of the one giving the advice. There may be a moment where your life is overwhelming and someone comes to you in excitement or discouragement. Then, you tell them to pray about it out of lack of energy due to your own circumstances. As hard as this may be, considering I often fail to do this or recognize this situation, be vulnerable. If someone is coming to you for genuine advice, I imagine you are involved enough in their life to tell them you do not have the capacity to emotionally process something with them at that moment. I can tell you that setting this boundary will help both sides. I often have had to navigate this with my mom. Finding a time that is good for the both of us to unwind and talk through things that are heavy has helped and strengthened our relationship immensely. Yet, it takes time and commitment to honor the other person in the relationship, and to say the least, it is a learning curve.

The second piece of advice I grew up hearing was, if it is God's will, it will happen. This is another 'truth' that does not portray fully what most people intend for it to mean. Again, I believe most people do say these pieces of advice with pure intentions, but there is so much more to the topic of God's will than just 'it will happen'. Don't get me wrong it *will* happen, but it is not so cookie cutter. God's will is beautiful, intentional, and unique for each and every one of us. He intends for us to live life and live life abundantly.

John 10:10

The thief comes only to steal and kill and destroy; I have come that they may have life, and have it to the full.

He wants to see us prosper, but that does not mean His will is a cakewalk. Just as God promises us abundant life, Jesus also recognized that there will be troubles in this life. He knows that because of the sin we committed, we live in a broken world, and that is going to cause troubles in this world.

John 16:33

I have told you these things, so that in me you may have peace. In this world you will have trouble. But take heart! I have overcome the world.

Coming back to discerning God's will. God is a God of movement, He works wonders, He moves mountains, and sets your path before you. He is building the road of your life, brick by brick.

Imagine this: You go through one of the toughest seasons of your life, whatever it may look like. Maybe homelessness. Maybe unwanted divorce or infidelity. Maybe sickness or disease Whatever a hard season looks like in your life. Now, shamefully, I can attest to this. I bet you, just as I would, will pray more in this season than any other. It is in our nature. We pray in the bad times; we cry for our God to come alongside and take it all away. I've been there. I've prayed those prayers. Now continue to imagine what you would do in each and every one of these situations. Ideally, if someone was homeless, they would try to find a job or even a place to stay warm or out of the weather. If someone was sick, they would talk to doctors and see what can be done.

Now stay with me and let's zone in on one example, sickness. Someone who is sick or terminally ill, would go to doctors, plural. They seek advice, but not only do they seek advice, they take the actions advised. They take a step. No doctor is allowed to force a patient into treatment. The initiative lies within the patient.

That is the concept: taking the step. We as Christians get so inherently caught up in waiting on the Lord, and 'letting His will just happen'. That personally, I believe we miss opportunities that would display the goodness of God in our lives.

This feeds into another well-known quote in our Christian culture: "God will open the doors if it is meant to happen". This in and of itself is completely true, but again there is more to it. If someone opens the door for you, you don't just stand there. Well, I mean most people don't. You take the step through the door. To this day, I have never had someone open a door for me, grab my hand,

and yank me through. In transparency, if anyone did do this, there would be a bit of an issue.

In the same way, God will open doors, but He is not going to yank you through. He requires you to take steps. Even more so, there are times when He has the door right in front of you from the beginning, but there are also times when He asks you to walk up by yourself.

My point is that God is not a genie. Prayer is powerful, and it is a beautiful aspect of faith, but so is taking action. We serve a God who moves. He wants us to move. If every Christian in the world sat in their home and prayed for the world to be saved, the world would never come to know Jesus. If you were in the room when your significant other got diagnosed with a disease and was told what action steps to take, you would hold them accountable and want them to take those steps. The same amount of accountability needs to be held within our churches. We need to share our God dreams, we need to pray about them, and then we need to move forward, because in reality if we are not moving, we are not even giving God the opportunity to close or open the door.

James 2:26

As the body without the spirit is dead, so faith without deeds is dead.

So I challenge you to take that first step, and oftentimes, that means being vulnerable and sharing your God dream with someone, but I can promise you it will all be worth it. It will also often validate whether or not it is truly what God intends for you. If it is, God will open the doors. If it isn't, He will redirect your path. Either way, He is with you.

In lieu of this topic, I will share a personal experience where I saw this come to life. When I first decided to write this book, I thought it was a whim. I have thought about writing before, and have even applied for writing jobs, but it never truly was an opportunity I followed through with. I went about my life as usual, but I kept hearing the whisper in my quiet times. So then I started, but in my spirit, I was still doubtful. I wrote the first chapter and a half and started seeing God speak to me through my words. This got the ball rolling, and I got excited, but I enjoyed the fact that no one knew, because I didn't want any expectations on myself. Then one day, I was on the phone with a friend, who was studying abroad in Europe. She has been such a blessing in my life, and we were just catching up about life, at the moment I felt like I should tell her. While on the phone, I wrestled with the Holy Spirit, I did not want to tell anyone, but God had other plans. So I told her. I did not know why. We are close, don't get me wrong, but I am close with several people, and I had no desire to tell anyone, not even my family. Yet, God knew I needed the confirmation, because when I told her, she noted that her mom had a book published. She told me she was excited, listened to what I had so far, and encouraged me that she would help with the process.

Will that happen? I have no clue, but in that moment, it was what I needed to encourage me to keep going. God works, He sees our heart, and He has a plan. Later that week, I was reading back in my journals, and found a note that said 'write a book' from months prior. This again was confirmation.

All of that being said, I would have never gotten this far if I had not started writing and seeing God work, and I would not have kept going if I had not talked to my friend or read back into my journal. So just as much as this book is God's will, He loves us so much that He invites us into the process. It is so humbling that a God so powerful allows us to work with Him, He is so much more than we could ever ask for.

Take that step.

WORDS OF TRUTH

Truth has become less and less clear the more our society progresses or in some cases digresses. Truth used to be validated by many and accepted by all. Now the truth has seemingly become subjective. I personally have opinions on this, but to some extent they do not matter. If I were to sit here and spill my thoughts solely on what I think is the truth, that would be as subjective as our society. The fact of the matter is that truth is derived from the Word, and the Word alone.

This is an important idea that I think every Christian needs to come to terms with when wanting to discern their calling, or what they are hearing from God. I think that we can all get caught up in our own subtle thoughts of what truth is and that can seep into our view of what God is telling us, or asking us to do. This could lead to misconception and lack of clarity when it comes to discerning His voice.

When approaching the Word, it is essential to go into the Scripture with the intent of reading in context (more on this next). This reduces the chances of misinterpretation and neglects the tendency to go to the Word to back up the truth you want to defend.

This is not always easy because it does require time and commitment, but it is worth it. It is worth digging into the Word when you think God is speaking, it is worth practicing discernment, it is worth building a community that will help you do these things. Yet, anything worthwhile takes time.

Circling back to words of truth, I am going to bring it all into perspective with a verse, but first, let me give you the context. In John 14, Jesus is speaking to His disciples about how He is going to be leaving them. As any person would be concerned about a close friend, the disciples are asking Him questions about what He means. Then comes the following.

John 14:5-7

Thomas said to him, "Lord, we don't know where you are going, so how can we know the way?"

Jesus answered, "I am the way and the truth and the life. No one comes to the Father except through me. If you really knew me, you would know my Father as well. From now on, you do know him and have seen him."

In simple terms, Jesus is truth. Yet, that is incredibly vague and does not give much personal application for one to walk away with. Nonetheless, it does show how beautifully simple life can be. Replicate Jesus to get to the Father. So where do words of truth come in?

That is where I would like to make a few points. First, one thing I have found which is age old, but tried and true, is asking if Jesus would have done it. This seems child-like, but in a sense, it is what this verse compels us to consider. He is the way, so the way to the Father is believing in Him and trusting Him to help us become more like Him.

Secondly, the larger picture of the disciples' lives brings relief for guilt. Oftentimes, we try to discern God's voice in our life, and we mess up, or we fall back into habitual sin. This then leads us into a guilt that is not of the Lord. Yet, the disciples all made mistakes, some of His closest friends struggled with doubt and denial. As well, they also struggled with sin issues. This is relieving in a sense as it shows that we are not expected to discern His Words perfectly every single time. Even more so, it shows that there is an abundance of grace for when we do mess up.

CONTEXT

The question: Will you go to Ecuador? The context: none. Let me elaborate. I was sitting at my university, studying when a friend of a friend came up to me and asked this question. I was confused, especially considering I had never really talked to this guy. There was no initial context. No information, no background, nothing. To answer based on the one question would have been unwise and quite concerning. I did say yes after more information, but this is often the level of context we are comfortable with when getting into the Word.

Based on one question, there was no chance that I was making a decision. Yet, when I have a singular question I quickly look to the Word, find what seems to be an applicable verse to my life situation at that very moment and keep going. This is concerning. The Word is so rich. Rich with a wealth of endless knowledge that is living. To simply 'control f' the Word to find what we want to hear bars us from the intimate relationship we so innately desire with the Father.

In my years of friendships and companions and all types of relationships, there are few people that I genuinely know deeply. Few that I genuinely believe will be there for me no matter what. People that I know care for me potentially even more than I care for myself. Yet, the beautiful (somewhat annoying) attribute that every one of these people share is authenticity. Authenticity within our relationship means telling me what I do not always want to hear. This authenticity has held them to a standard of putting my best interest before gratifying my mood or plans. They have told me that I was wrong, that I needed to apologize in a situation, or that I was not taking care of myself. All good things, because without this authenticity, I would not believe that these people would be there for me no matter what.

That said, when we cherry pick Scripture, we do not show up for authentic conversations with the One who truly does know what is best for us. Reading Scripture in context allows for us to have those moments like you would with an old friend. Moments of comfort, moments of conviction, and moments of calling you not to give up. This is beautiful, this is a true relationship, this is priceless.

WHAT CAN WE DO

It is not always easy, but I plead with you to just start somewhere. Read a passage, read a chapter, or read a book of the Bible. Just read in a larger sum than one verse. Pray for Him to reveal His heart and have an open mind towards what He could be saying to you. There are so many different ways to study. There are systems, plans, methods, and more. They are good but can be overwhelming. Yet, we serve a beautiful Lord who meets us where we are at. He knows our hearts and wants to be in a relationship with us. He will meet you wherever you are.

When we start to be intentional with our time in the Word, grasp context, and pursue difficult conversations with the One who made us, we will inevitably start to become more like Jesus. We will start reflecting the One who loved others, who knew His purpose, and who pursued the heart of the Father wholeheartedly. Just think what the Church would start to look like if we all pursued our communal calling of being more like Christ.

CHAPTER 4

LOOKING BACK

INADEQUACY

This is not easy. Inadequacy is still a massive part of my story. I pray for the day there is no longer the lingering feeling of having to prove myself. I am well aware that it is self-imposed. I have walked through seasons of life where I felt loved, fulfilled by the Spirit, and purposeful. Yet, I would be lying if I said that I have completely resolved this issue.

Inadequacy is defined as 'the state of being inadequate which is further defined as not enough, or insufficient' ("Inadequate"). It is so apparent to me that the Father loves me. His love is more real to me than potentially anything in this life. Nonetheless, I find a disconnect between the love of the Father and the feeling of adequacy. I grew up, as mentioned, being good at things. This led to me expecting myself to be good at things. It really is not anyone else's expectations, but my own. Some may think- just give yourself a break. Many have said that to me, but it, like most things, is easier said than done.

Over the years, I mainly struggled with the feeling of inadequacy in school. Despite being confident in school, doubt crept in. The same happened with sports, especially once I got to high school. Yet, God walked me through that. He held my hand and taught me that it is Him and I. He walked with me as I fought to keep imposing unrealistic standards on myself. He showed me it is okay to say no to too many commitments, to let go of the bad grade, and to know that sports do not define me.

Nevertheless, in complete transparency, I am writing this section amidst finals week of junior year. I have had some severe highs and lows so far this week, and it is only Tuesday. Yesterday I found myself inundated with pressure. I get into these moments where it's hard to breathe. In my head, I know it is all going to be okay, I recite the scriptures, I pray, and I listen to music. I am learning how to handle it. Yet, this has led to a new flavor of feeling inadequate, and it is being a Christian that struggles with anxious thoughts. I tell myself to get over it, that others have it worse, and that if I would just trust more, Jesus would take it away. But that is so far from the truth.

In essence, there is some truth within these statements, but the statements as a whole are not true. Others do have it worse than me. I have lived a blessed life, and I will be the first to own that in a more than grateful way. Yet, my life circumstances do not invalidate my struggle. David, the King, the One after God's heart, the one the nations praised, and enemies trembled before, struggled. He was rich, he could have any woman, and he had close friends. Despite all of that, you can see in the Psalms that he had his highs and lows and the beauty of it all is that there is no condemnation that follows. He is still considered the King, the One after God's heart, the one the nations praised, and enemies trembled before, even with his struggles.

This comes to show that God does not expect perfection, he expects obedience. He expects us to chase after Him wholeheartedly. He expects us to mess up. Even before we do so, He has provided grace sufficient enough to cover that sin. It is beautiful. These are the thoughts I need to be reminding myself of in those anxious moments.

A song called Jireh written by Elevation Worship and Maverick City Music says, "Wasn't holding you up, so there's nothing I can do to let you down" ("Jireh"). These very words have broken down a majority of the inadequacy feelings in my life. As mentioned, I am still walking through that, but just as those words have helped me, I encourage you to listen to music that uplifts your heart. I pray that God breaks down your walls of inadequacy because you are His beloved.

GUILT

Some say guilt is from God and shame is of the devil. I do not know if I believe this. I think that conviction comes from the Lord. I do not think that God would ever ask us to live in regret or guilt or shame ridden state. His goodness is too good to let that be the case.

Guilt played a big role in my teenage years. Guilt of something I could never change. Guilt is synonymous with regret for me in this situation. My brothers are significantly older than me. They were raised differently than I was and as a kid I do not think I fully understood that. All I knew is that in school and church I was being told of this "Good News" that we were supposed to tell everyone about. It is good news, and it should be shared, but again, at this stage in life I was just one of those Christians that was yelling Jesus at everyone. This especially meant my brothers because they mean so much to me. As a kid, that made the most sense, I had heard of this beautiful, wonderful gift that we are given freely, and that we can share. With this I knew I needed to share it with them, because my heart so desired for them to know of this beautiful gift we are given. This, at least in my perspective, drove them further and further from Christ, and even more so away from me.

I wholeheartedly believe that they love me, but I know that as long as I love Jesus there will be division. For years, I blamed myself, I hated young Erin for being so forward and shoving my newfound beliefs on them. It became even more real after a few conversations about God.

I believe there is a redemption story written for both of them. For me, I came to learn that it was not my fault. God has a plan and even in our stubbornness and failures He will work. I did not push my brothers out of His reach. I do not believe I was completely right in the situation, if anything I will be the first to admit that I did not go about it the right way, but my heart was in the right place as much as a young kid's heart can be. God saw that and still sees that. I look back and just as much as those moments of me telling them about Jesus excessively make me cringe, I also remember the nights I laid in bed pleading with God to bring them to Him. I remember the gut-wrenching sobs of sheer desperation I used to cry as a child, telling Him that I would take their place in Hell if He would just let them into heaven. This is something God revealed to me over my later teenage years. First, He made me aware of the guilt I was carrying. A burden that wasn't mine to bear. Then He reminded me of the depth of His love. He reminded me He is the God of the impossible. And that He has a plan.

This guilt I carried, subconsciously for a while, and then consciously for some time as well, was not of Christ. He did not go to the cross for me to walk with unnecessary burdens. He has freedom in store. That is the beauty of serving a God without limits, because despite our failures He can still redeem those we hurt.

SHAME

Have you ever seen someone do something and thought "Wow they are completely shameless". I have. Sometimes it is because it is an act I just would not do, or because it is bold and unapologetic. It can be a bad thing, but it can also be a good thing. So what does it look like to be shameless? A lot of minds, like mine, take this in a negative connotation. A way of life that is far from God, a way of life that flaunts every aspect. Yet, I want to look at it differently. Shameless, shame - less. The word in itself has no connotation. It is actually quite straightforward: to be without shame.

To address what it may look like to live shamelessly; I think it is important to address what it looks like to live with shame first. There's a lot to be said about living with shame. I believe every person has walked with shame for some part of their life. I did. Mine was a fun mixture of self-hatred and shame. It also looked different in different seasons of life. It looked like being ashamed of my body, being ashamed of what I thought was inadequacy, being ashamed of my privilege, and many other forms. I am sure that a few things come to mind when you think of shame. I really struggled with my body image through high school. Now I look back and realize that there was absolutely nothing to be ashamed of. In all honesty, aside from when I was a gymnast, I was in the best shape of my life in high school. It still did not matter because I was not built like most of the cross-country girls. This was a completely irrational shame that weighed me down for years. The shame tainted my view of myself so much that it affected my world view. Shame will do that. It is not a concentrated effect on your life. It seeps into every aspect. The shame of my body then resulted in fear and shame of inadequacy. I felt inadequate in school, as I was in a very different atmosphere than what I had grown up in. This bled into feeling inadequate in sports. Lastly, after my first mission trip, I felt completely ashamed of my environment and the privilege I had of growing up in the United States. I felt as though I did not deserve it at all, I did not understand why there were people starving while I was looking in a full refrigerator complaining that we had nothing to eat. I was completely ashamed.

Do not get me wrong, there are subtle truths in these. It was true that I did not look like some of the other girls, it was true that I was surrounded by peers who challenged me more than what I was used to, and it is true that I am blessed beyond measure for the beautiful life God has given me. That is why it is so easy to fall into shame, because the devil dresses up lies to make shame a little more difficult to detect.

It's toxic. Shame can be consuming. Please do not take my language as invalidating. I am still walking through different flavors of shame in my life, and it is not easy. However, it is one thing, like sin, that I believe is universal. Why? Because shame and sin are the devil's two greatest devices. It is quite devious if you think about it. The devil convinces us to sin, and then when we want to own up to our faults or get healing from our past, he fills us with shame. Only to keep us on the path away from God. This is not what God intended. This is not what God has in store for you. He has freedom in store. He has a history of breaking chains of shame and guilt, and He can do it. He is in the mending business. Whatever that may look like for you, maybe it is the need for a mended home, relationship, body image, or whatever has caused you to carry shame. No matter what it looks like for you specifically, He can deliver you from it and there is freedom on the other side.

LIES

There is some sort of youthfulness that surrounds lying. A lot of us grew up tantalizing our friends and siblings about their pants catching on fire. I think that some people, including myself, correlate lying with youth. After spending time with kids, it is obvious to see when they are lying. Their faces say it all. The irony in all of it is that this is how the Father views us. He sees right through it. Comparably, people also recognize that oftentimes, kids don't benefit from lying, neither do we. We try to justify lying to the point that we end up confused and stressed. As soon as a lie is told, a little bundle of shame starts to form in us. I am not going to tell you not to lie. You've most likely been told that since day one and are going to do what you want. Yet, I do want to touch on believing lies. This has been an uphill battle for me, and I think that it is important to address.

There is a simplicity in recognizing lies that children tell. "Did you wash your hands?" "Uhhhh, yeah". No, they did not. What if the lies are more subtle? What if the lies are dressed up in constructive criticism, or just criticism? What if the lies are from people you hold dear? Then it isn't so easy to recognize. Even more so, it is hard to recognize how much they are affecting you.

I've seen this multiple times, personally and in my friends' lives. It all lies within the subtleties, as cliche as that may sound. I also find that we as Christians are very guilty of this too. The reality of having a conversation and coming away completely deflated happens more often than not. Why? Because we lace our conversations with demeaning idiosyncrasies that tear each other down. The saddest part is that we may be so habitually used to this that we do not even notice it. So what does it look like? Before we get to that, let me put out a little disclaimer. Truth is uncomfortable, but often makes you have revelation in your life. This is not the type of conversation I am talking about. I am talking about lies laced in our words that can demean and hurt immensely. An example for me was in a recent conversation, I was sharing my excitement of what God has in store for me. I have been praying for years for this, and was simply sharing some revelation and newfound excitement, and openness towards where God is leading me. In return, the conversion changed quickly to trusting God day by day. This completely deflated my excitement and made me shut down in a way.

This example shows how little lies can be insinuated through our words. It is not a full lie. Trusting God day by day is imperative. Yet, I feel like as Christians we can get caught up in trying to say the perfect God honoring thing. This, as I have witnessed it, and practiced it, shows that we are lacking listening skills. We are so focused on nit picking each other's lives, to try and spur each other on that we end up focusing on what to say rather than what the person is sharing.

Another example that I became aware of on my mission trip to Georgia was relating stories. Yes, I do believe there is a time and a place to share and relate on certain levels. But have you ever poured your heart out to someone, only to be met with I know how you feel when this happened to me… and suddenly you are supporting them.

This is not necessarily a lie, but this is something that we struggle with when it comes to listening to each other.

Going back to my first example, I can tell you that I shared the same excitement with another person, and they told me they were happy for the growth and can see the excitement all over my face. This is more of what we need to be like. I am not stating that I need to be validated, I am saying that we need to build each other up. Learning to read situations means not necessarily encouraging delusions, but rather being authentic about people's excitement. We are so quick to comfort people when they are down but fail to celebrate them when they are excited. I can tell of a time where someone did this well. I am an engineering student and took one of my board exams. I studied for a month and passed. When I told one of my closest friends, she cried. I truly have never felt more appreciated and encouraged in my life. To see someone truly step into celebration with me was something I will always remember.

Our lies that come out of our mouths when someone else is sharing, often bleeds the colors of our own discontentment or insecurity. So, my challenge to you is to watch what you say and take note of what might make you let out a well-intended lie. Then reflect on that. Reflect on that aspect of your own life and ask God to revive that part of your life.

For me, I remember I once was in a conversation with a friend about missions, and she was about to apply to go on a long-term trip. I honestly don't remember if I verbalized anything. I may have said, "Well, have you really thought about it?" or "Maybe you should pray about it more." When in reality she had thought about it, she had prayed, and she was following God's heart. When it came down to it the truth of the matter was jealousy. Jealousy because she was up and going on the mission field and I was still here going to school. That is the kind of situation I am talking about.

Not every situation where you ask someone to pray about something is bad, but sometimes we dress up our own flaws in Christianese and project them on others. So just be aware, challenge yourself to grow, and ask God to convict you when your advice to others isn't rooted in Him.

On the other hand, do not let someone saying something to you change the course God set you on. There are times in our lives that God uses others to speak to us, but there are also times in our lives that the devil speaks to us through others. The devil does not want us to pursue Christ. In all reality, it makes sense that he would use others to discourage us. Even more so, he would use other Christians that we are quicker to believe. I would say that just like any other aspect of life, proceed with caution. Pray for discernment and walk in the Spirit. There will be discouragement, and that is okay, but letting it define your walk or change your heart towards the Father is not.

WHAT CAN WE DO

As Christians what can we do better in light of inadequacy, guilt, shame, and lies? The reality is that this chapter was mostly about introspective issues. Outside factors can play roles when it comes to feelings of inadequacy, guilt, and shame, but at the same time, it is something that we have to deal with in our hearts, and often with

God. Yet, if we are not taking care of ourselves, what is the likeliness of our outer actions reflecting Christ well? How can we have overwhelming burdens in our own lives, and still go out and help the world bear theirs? My encouragement would be to step into the discomfort of finding the root of the inadequacy, shame, and guilt in your life. Press into the realities God may be trying to reveal in your life, because the more in tune we are with Him, the clearer our reflection of Him to others will be.

CHAPTER 5

SINGLENESS

WHAT THE WORLD SAYS

Marriage is the goal. You are valued depending on your marital status. You are getting older, you should find a man. Your friends are married with families, when do you expect to be on that level? It will come when you are not looking.

OR

You are a strong independent woman. You are equal to a man. You can find everything you need within yourself. You are the answer. Your own desires and dreams are all that matter. Prioritize yourself no matter what.

OR

Maybe if you had a boyfriend, other guys would respect you. A boyfriend can just be a fun time. Let yourself have a little fun. It is okay to have a fling, if that is all it is. Just let go, no one is ever going to live up to your standards.

All things I have heard from all types of people, all ages, all belief systems, and both genders. The question is about singleness. This is what seems to be the expectations in one way or another.

One person thinks that you are only validated if you are in a relationship. Another that your goal as a young woman should be to get married. Another that women should be independent and completely dismiss the necessity of a man. This is sad. It is a hard reality that the world has every expectation and when it comes to singleness it seems that being single is never an acceptable situation. Let alone being happy in singleness.

The only valid reason for singleness is to be completely and utterly focused on yourself in order to further yourself and your career. This seems to be the new trend. We went from women belonging in the kitchen to women being so independent that needing a man is a weakness.

It is a catch twenty two. Every person has an opinion. Singleness has been boiled down to two things: a season to endure or a time to focus solely on yourself. Yet, it is neither of those things.

WHAT THE WORD SAYS

What if the purpose of singleness is not to build endurance or become the most independent woman possible. What if the purpose of singleness is to find your identity in Christ.

Let me go on a slight tangent for a moment. There is a beauty in the advancements that technology has brought us. Honestly, it is not just technology, it is our western culture in general. Our culture, in my eyes, can be summed up quite easily. A people that desires more while getting lost in excess. We are lost in our own lives. We have come to terms with a severe lack of silence. In fact, to me it seems a lot of us are uncomfortable with silence. I was, and I used to avoid it at all costs. This bids the fear of singleness.

Quietness and singleness do not always go hand in hand, but they often are more acquainted than quietness and relationships.

There is security in a relationship and that is a beautiful thing. Security of a person for you, a person who will listen, who is there and who holds a presence in your life. Yet, this beautiful and powerful attribute to living in a relationship is often misconstrued. It becomes a lifeline. This was not the intention; God did not make us complementary beings for the sole reason of only depending on one another. Rather He made both man and woman complementary with Himself. As well, man and woman can be complementary to each other, but they also can thrive on their own.

Singleness, unlike dating, is addressed in the Bible. Ironically, against the current view of singleness, it is highly esteemed in the Bible. It is even encouraged, as it was seen as an opportunity to serve God wholeheartedly. Also, marriage is highly esteemed and recognized as a beautiful relationship to be had. There is simply something to be said about the two. Singleness is beautiful and marriage is beautiful.

I believe the root of the sour taste of singleness is more so found within individuals. I find that people are afraid to be on their own, for the fear that they may not like who they are. Oftentimes, people counteract this by filling their life with relationships of all sorts to drown out the quietness that begs the question, "Who are you?". In my mind, the discontentment with singleness bleeds into life in two forms. One is discontentment when in a season of singleness due to a lack of firm knowledge of a person's identity in Christ. The other is envy or disbelief that single people can find in themselves - more so God - what others are so desperately longing for. The mixture of these two belief systems creates the unbiblical perspective that is so apparent today.

Another common chain I have seen in discontent singleness is the reality of those who live in the world searching to fill a void that a relationship never will. It can be somewhat cliche to say that they have a God sized hole in their heart, but it is true. When we long to be loved in a way that isn't humanly possible, it is interesting that we look to humans to do it. We crave unconditional love; we crave being known in full and loved despite our failures and shortcomings. Yet, it is often a missed connection that those who will do that are significant others. The reality is we are craving love. A love that only God has to offer.

SEASONAL

To me seasons are an ebb and flow. There is something so intriguing about a season that we just walked through or are looking forward to. We tend to live in one of two narratives: longing for what was or chasing what could be. This is applicable to just about every area of life. Not just relationship status.

The idea that being alone is possible is often soothed with the idea that it is temporary. If we have to be single, we settle in our minds that it is temporary, also referred to as a season. Often a season to endure rather than enjoy. The irony I have found is that people do recognize the value of singleness, but this often occurs in a moment of realization that they may never be single again. This refers back to the idea of longing for what was.

As much as I feel people don't want to recognize the reality of desiring to live in a different situation, we often do know it is true. So what does it look like to embrace seasonal singleness in a practical way? A heavy question with a valuable answer.

Before going on, I want to preface that I do not know all aspects of this answer. It to some degree is an incredibly individual experience that may look different for everyone. Yet, I do believe that every person will have to come to terms with the center of the solution being surrender. Surrender to a God who knows better. Surrender to a God who already knows your spouse, and if you will have one. Surrender by letting go of the reins. Again, great in theory, but what about practicality? Practically, a lot of people throw themselves into something to distract themselves from unfulfilled desires (myself included). Rather than this, I challenge you to bring it to God in prayer. He has a way of either removing the desire or bringing other aspects of life to the forefront in order to show that there is more in store. He will always want more for you. That is the beauty of serving a God who is not just a God but also a Father, and a friend.

Another aspect of singleness as a season is filling the desire for relationships in other ways. God calls us to community. He himself as a being begs the importance of community. He is three in one. He is the essence of community. Christ's start to ministry was finding community. He easily could have done it alone, He is God. Yet, He chose not to. He chose community.

I also want to take you on a thought process.

Mary, Martha, and Lazarus. Three close friends of Jesus. We read about the time Jesus is with Mary and Martha. He reprimands Martha for being too busy to be in His presence. We hear about their relationship and many know their names. Yet, the gravity of Jesus and Lazarus' relationship is heavier than most know. For some background, Lazarus dies... he is without breath, and buried. Mary and Martha send for Jesus, yet he does not go right away. Yes, He knows that He is going to raise Lazarus from the dead.

Nevertheless, put yourself in Jesus' shoes. Put yourself in that friendship. Christ walked into that friendship. The first moment He saw Lazarus, He knew how deep their relationship would be, how genuine the love. He knew in that first glance that Lazarus was going to die. He knew the first time the pain that Mary and Martha would go through seeing their brother die. He knew that He himself would feel the weight of the loss and weep. Yet, despite that reality, He still stepped into a sweet friendship with this set of siblings.

The gravity of losing a loved one is hard don't get me wrong, but watching someone you love dearly grieve is heartbreaking. Often this is so hard to watch because there is nothing you can do. There is something that we often do, potentially without realizing it, to protect ourselves from this type of pain. We don't let people in. We think we guard our hearts by letting people only reach the surface. The more distance we create the less it will hurt if something doesn't work out. As logical as that may seem, it leads to a life of painstaking loneliness. A type of painstaking loneliness I think is inadvertently associated with singleness. When the truth of the matter is that loneliness is sometimes produced rather than inflicted.

This is the beauty of finding community in a season of singleness. Community is where we get to see the heart of God in others. We get to see reflections of God's image that we don't bear. We get to be loved and love others. We get to pursue deep and vulnerable relationships that will help sustain our wellbeing. We get to do all these things; the question is if we actually will. I can promise you that pursuing community while single has been one of the most heartwarming experiences in my walk with God. Life is so meant to be done together, and the sooner you start pursuing that with or without a significant other, the more you will see the living, breathing heart of God.

AGAINST THE GRAIN

The Word is incredibly countercultural. Everything about it is countercultural. Jesus was one to find the least of these and help them. He was one to help those in need even if they were the lowest in society. Yet, you probably know that. You probably have heard that a million times to the point that it loses all power. Take a moment and paint this picture in your mind:

It is a beautiful day in New York City, the air is warm and there is a refreshing breeze wrapping the buildings. Your family goes on a day trip to see the sights and embrace the inner-city busyness. You are strolling down the street with your sister by your side, she's younger than you and has never been to the city before. She has been more excited for this trip than everyone else combined. Your parents take you to a truly New York pizza place, and you are on your way to see the Empire State Building. During this walk, you pass a homeless man, your sister stares, and you whisper to her, "Don't make eye contact". Go your way and have a wonderful rest of your day.

Normal for people to do, almost so normal that I never thought twice about it. I have always noticed homeless people, we all do. Yet, I have caught myself looking the other way. This is where Jesus differs from us all. Jesus didn't look the other way. He looked into their ever-human eyes and expressed his love by simply acknowledging their existence. That is true love, that is the power of serving the least of these.

In that scenario it is easy to see and accept that Christ was countercultural. It is something that we all recognize that we should strive for. A heart for others that acknowledges the hard moments. Nevertheless, in recognizing that we should aim to be more like Christ, we tend to pick and choose what attributes of Christ that we want to strive for. Humble: yes. Loving: yes. Influential: yes. Powerful: yes! Sacrificial: kind of. Subordinate: not completely but we try. Single: no comment. (Disclaimer: once again, I truly believe marriage is a beautiful gift from God that He would not have made if He did not desire us to partake in it). Nonetheless, Christ, the Son of God, made it through life without a spouse. Paul, a man who was radically in love with the Lord and taking the Gospel to the ends of the earth, made it through life without a spouse. Mind you, both Christ and Paul went through some gruesome trials and tribulations, and they made it through, why? Because their firm foundation was the Father. Singleness is a blessing. Singleness deepens the necessary dependance on the Lord that we all should be pursuing. Singleness gives space for growth in your walk unlike a relationship or marriage ever will.

Singleness is countercultural. Singleness requires courage, but more importantly singleness drives us to our knees in a way that the only One there to comfort us is our Creator. How intimate. How intentional. How wonderful that our Father leaves room for those experiences.

WHAT CAN WE DO

This is a bit interesting and different from the previous chapters. Meaning that what we can do may not seem as explicit. The simple solution is not for everyone to pursue singleness. Yet, there is a role every person can play in helping singleness not have the stigma it does, especially in Christian culture. What I believe we can do as brothers and sisters in Christ is inclusion. This goes hand in hand with the idea of community. The first thing we may want to work against is the thought that singles are not whole. Singles are equally valuable to the church body. Married couples can call singles into a community and vice versa. The beauty of this is that it brings fresh perspectives into relationships. I don't know about you, but some of the best advice I have received is from people I would have least expected in incredibly different places in life than I. This is because oftentimes, someone else looking in may have a fresh and new perspective. This bids us to reach out to others and be in a community that is diverse, because while having people that are relatable and in the same season of life is wonderful, so is having others that aren't.

Another step I believe we can take as singles is to see it as an opportunity not a waiting period. As I mentioned earlier in the chapter, there is space when you are single to pursue Christ and have extended time with God. It is a gracious gift in my perspective. So a shift in perspective may be what we all truly need when it comes to singleness.

CHAPTER 6

MORE THAN ENOUGH

DENOUNCING LIES

Little did I know what God was going to walk me through when I outlined this book. It was August of 2022 when I sat down and outlined the chapters of this book. I also want to note that I did not write this book chronologically. Since I had the outline, I would write here and there for different chapters. Somewhat picking and choosing what I wanted to approach, but each time God challenged my heart and drew me to write about what I often needed to hear myself. It is currently July of 2023 and God has been working overtime specifically in the department of denouncing lies in my life.

I will share more of that in a bit. First, I want to talk about subtlety. Jim Collins once wrote "Good is the enemy of great" ("Collins"). From that I believe the enemy uses subtlety to counteract what we believe should be obvious. Meaning, no one goes around living life overly cognizant of the fact that they are living in lies. We often walk around with the delusion that we are walking in freedom. Why? Because the lies are subtle, not always warranted from a traumatic experience, but often a series of subconscious beliefs that we start to accept as truth.

To demonstrate this point, here goes nothing. In complete transparency, this is still an ongoing topic in my walk with God. I am so desperately far from being freed from this, but the first step is recognition. I am a person's person, a people pleaser, and a highly extroverted introvert. I love time to myself, but I love socializing especially when I can serve others in some capacity. Again, no crazy red flags, or so I thought. Over the last four months, I have met some friends who I truly value. They have shown me what it means to live purposely alongside a community who truly has your back. This has brought some previously subtle issues to light in my life. I thrive in social aspects when I am the one giving because for the longest time, that is all I knew. I truly inhabited most friendships with the perspective that it is a one-way street. I am there for them whenever, wherever, however they need me. Yet, oftentimes this led to me feeling more alone than anything. I was always the one carrying the burdens for everyone around me. I reconciled this with the idea that we are meant to care for people, we are meant to take up our cross, we are meant to be a shoulder to cry on.

Then I walked into this community. A place so genuine. A place full of listening ears that authentically cared for what I was going through. It was, in all honesty, utterly foreign. I was completely out of my comfort zone, and in some aspects absolutely terrified. I recognized this, and then really struggled to open up to these people. Yet, it wasn't until a few months later that the lie that was becoming less and less subtle became a blaring siren that I could not ignore. I genuinely believed that I was unlovable.

An apparent lie. A lie that even now I still almost laugh when saying it because I know it isn't true, but to some respect it has grasped my heart to the point that it isn't just a thought it is a feeling. It is a genuine belief that I have / had about myself. These are the lies we need to diligently seek out and denounce. As I said before, these lies are often a series of subconscious thoughts that we start to accept as truth. I had a white picket fence childhood. Probably one of the most typical American upbringings out there. I was not neglected or put through the system. I was loved by my parents who are still married to this day. I have siblings who have always loved and protected me. Yet here I was sitting in Long Beach Island at a discipleship program bawling my eyes out when God revealed the overwhelming reality that He loved me. Yes, again something I knew. God loves me, but in that moment, it was coupled with the realization of the lie that I believed I wasn't capable of being loved.

The opposite of the truth. The truth of the matter is that I am loved. Loved by God, loved by family, loved by friends. I am loved in all types of capacities. Yet, it doesn't resonate. Growing up, I was easily good at things as I have mentioned. I can often figure something out rather quickly and maybe not master it, but at least become proficient. This resulted in being a well-rounded child. I was smart and athletic, and both of those were showcased in my small private school. As it is said by Rudolph Dreikurs, "Children are keen observers, but poor interpreters" ("Dreikurs"). I have now come to recognize that growing up the praise and success I received and gained was not the root of the issue. That was a result of those around me being proud of me and hard work. Yet, as a kid, I interpreted it as success warranted love. Hence, lack of success warranted disappointment. This is far from the truth. Nonetheless over the years this subconsciously was how I operated. I saw myself as a producer. I had to achieve things and be the one constantly giving to be worth something in a relationship. I lack boundaries for the sake of trying to please those around me. I aim to serve at the cost of sitting in the reality that Christ loves me whether or not I complete my to - do list.

I share this to show that lies can be so deeply rooted in your life without you knowing. Even more so, these lies do not have to be rooted in trauma to exist. Mine was rooted in praise and misinterpretation. Yet, even the ounces of freedom I have gained from this in the last few months has been a weight off my shoulders in a life changing way.

The reality is that you are more than enough, we are not worthy of His love, but that doesn't negate us from being recipients of it. There is so much freedom on the other side of recognizing lies. This is because the opposite of a lie is the truth and the truth of who you are is who God made you to be. God made us so intricately and intentionally. When He knit us together in our mother's wombs, He did not sprinkle in lies just for the fun of it. These lies were never meant to be an integral part of our lives. He has so much more.

Psalms 139:13

For you created my inmost being; you knit me together in my mother's womb.

WAITING

Like the season of singleness, the season of waiting has quite a distasteful reputation. I don't think anyone inherently desires to be in a season of waiting.

Hear me out. The picture I feel like I often relate to a season of waiting is one of being in a dentist office waiting room. The walls are a muted shade of blue, the floors reflect the fluorescent lighting, and the time between sitting down and hearing your name typically feels like at least a century. This type of waiting is terrible and to some degree warrants the reputation that waiting has. But what if that isn't the image we correlate with a season of waiting? What if by simply changing our perspective we recognize the value and beauty in waiting. What if we picture it as the month of December instead. Meaning, picture a young couple with a five-year-old and a three-year-old. The month of December is full of excitement and energy. There is just that Christmas ambiance in the air, which is fun and exciting, yet December is also one of the busiest seasons. Finding time to get presents, containing the kids' energy, and also making sure Christmas is all they want it to be for their little ones. Then comes Christmas Eve. Everything the month of December entailed is finished and now they wait to see their kids enjoy what they have worked hard for. This is how we should view a season of waiting.

The difference is that there is excitement, purpose, and enjoyment. All of which leads to a sincere fulfillment when the season is over. This would bring revival into our in between's. This would cause exponential growth, and even more efficiency in seasons that aren't a period of waiting. This is how I will be viewing the seasons of waiting.

In retrospect, this is what some of my season of waiting for the past three years has looked like. I would say the first year and a half felt closer to a dentist office waiting room. I was shaken, I went from planning to move overseas to being in lockdown. This was followed by a lot of alone time. This did lead to some growth in my personal walk with God, but my outlook on life was definitely not one of contentment. Then around my sophomore year spring, I joined the

Navigators and stepped into community. I also found a new home church and was able to start serving again. In a lot of aspects, life was being revived and so was I. I truly started passionately living for the season I was in. To this day, I am. I love my life. I have hard times, and do not get me wrong I am looking forward to Christmas, but this seasonal month of December is so fruitful.

HE IS FAITHFUL WHO HAS CALLED

Oh man what a time to be writing about this. First, this book is about 11 months in the making. The faithfulness of God is the fact that I outlined these chapters without knowing how much He was going to walk me through in the midst of writing this book.

Anyway, for about four years now, I have been completely enamored by God's faithfulness. He has given me so many reasons to believe. In a recent Bible study, we were asked "What makes you convinced of your faith?" My answer was His faithfulness. Because of how many times God has shown up for me. Then the next person said, "I agree, I've just seen too much". This really resonated with me. God truly will open up and show up when we give Him space to, and even when we don't.

In all honesty, I could go on and on about stories where God showed up. Where He did the impossible in my life, where He was utterly encapsulating. Yet, the gravity of those stories will not necessarily resonate with everyone. Instead, I am going to take a moment to consider our role in God's faithfulness.

A weird turn of events, I am going to be honest. In a section of God's faithfulness, I originally had no intention of talking about us.

Yet, I genuinely believe the only way to know the gravity of God's faithfulness is to experience it. As much as I wish I could explain the surreal moments where God reveals how faithful He is, I can't. There is no language on this earth to explain Him in full.

What do we have to do to experience this immaculate faithfulness? Well, there is no recipe, or one direct solution, but still every single person is sufficient to receive His faithfulness. There is nothing that can disqualify you from the blessing of our faithful Father. The fact of the matter is that we often are too busy to recognize God's faithfulness in our lives.

For a moment, think back five years. Where did you think you would be by now? If it is where you are, that is God's faithfulness. If it isn't, that is also God's faithfulness. He has a way of working through everything. He is so overly intelligent that our decisions can't derail His plan. He is aware that we have free will, yet He can still use you if you take a wrong turn. Our God is one that has infinite redirections in store, He is sovereign and will pursue your heart no matter how far you roam. Even more so, our decisions will not drive Him away from being faithfully by our side. He will always go before you, walk behind you, and be beside you.

Again, I feel that there is a certain stigma to knowing God's faithfulness. Some seem to equate their faith to how faithful God is. That if we have more faith, God is more faithful. If we lack faith, God lacks faithfulness. This is so far from the truth. In fact, Jesus addresses this in the New Testament. He mentions that if you have faith the size of a mustard seed, you can move mountains. For reference, a mustard seed weighs about 0.00007 ounces (0.002 grams). That is quite small. In fact, that is negligible in most mathematical senses. So even your mustard seed of faith is more than enough.

Simply put, God's faithfulness does not depend on ours. We may have the most negligible amount of faith, and He will still show up and show out.

DON'T BE STAGNANT

So where does that leave us? Where does the space between our faith and God's faithfulness become a space where God-size stories are written? This is where I believe we must reconcile that faith without action is dead.

James 2:17

In the same way, faith by itself, if it is not accompanied by action, is dead.

There is no action that can make or break your admittance to heaven. Salvation is salvation. There are no ifs, ands, or buts about that. Yet, I do believe that God invites us into a family and kingdom. With that invitation also comes a call. A call to be kingdom minded. A call to reach the lost, love the unlovable, and help those in need. These are all great things. Yet, in some aspects these are actions that are simply attained. It is very evident if someone goes and feeds the poor. Even tangible I would say. Yet, I believe that movement in one's life, and even growth in one's life isn't solely outlined by the ministry achieved.

That may seem counterintuitive. Shouldn't Christians be loving one another, feeding the sick, and helping the poor? Yes. But

Christians should also be flooding heaven with prayers, actively memorizing Scripture, and living as God's promises are true. I would, sadly, assume that many Christians would agree that they are living in the truth of God's promises, yet they may not actually know the promises. I am guilty of this. I have said it, I have believed that God's promises are true, yet I could not necessarily put language to them. Language being Scriptures. Imagine if we put as much effort into knowing God's Word as we do to doing His work. Yes, churches need to be run, logistics need to be talked through, and finances must be overseen, but what if we started seeing all of those ministry opportunities through the lens of the promises of God. What if our outward ministry became just a fraction of our walk with God.

Take this with a grain of salt, but maybe if we had leaders that believed Isaiah 8:10, ministries would push through opposition (with discernment of course). They would recognize that the God who led the Israelites is the same God who stands by our side.

Isaiah 8:10

Devise your strategy, but it will be thwarted; propose your plan, but it will not stand, for God is with us.

Holding onto the promises of the Word does not guarantee lack of stagnancy, but rather will help in seasonal lows. There will always be ebbs and flows in life. Even if you are actively memorizing Scripture, serving, and studying the Word. There is a beauty to the fact that life isn't level. Life is always in a state of constant change. As stated earlier in the book, it truly depends on what you do in the differing seasons of your life. Look at waiting as Christmas Day, look at a stagnant season as just that, a season. Sometimes I think that my relationship with God is exempt from my emotions. I find myself being disappointed that I am not at a spiritual ten out of ten at all times. Yet, the reality is no relationship is always at a ten out of ten. The beauty of a relationship is the enjoyment in great seasons weighs so much more when hard seasons have been walked through. This is the same with God. Closeness is built in difficulty.

WHAT CAN WE DO

This is all fine and dandy, but what do you do when you feel utterly convinced that you are stuck in a stagnant season and there is no way out. I honestly can't tell you. If I knew I would. The only thing I can say is in these seasons, consistency is key. Not feeling like you're getting anything from the Word? Keep reading. Not feeling like your prayers are being heard? Keep praying. These are the spiritual disciplines that will carry you through. There are moments in time that it feels like God is far, but He isn't. The conundrum is that often when we start to feel this, we fall out of our spiritual disciplines, the very habits that are sustaining our relationship with God. Then there is truly a disparity of time with God in your life and the distance is there.

My only advice would be to try to keep consistency even in the dry spells. Try to pursue Him when it is the last thing you want to do. Hold onto His promises, pray them over your life and the lives of those around you. Pray big prayers and expect even bigger answers. Use what little faith you must see what a God that hasn't changed will do. He is the God of Abraham. The God who asked him to leave, in order to make him the father of many nations. He is the God of

Isaac. The God who prepared a sacrifice when Isaac's life was on the line.

He is the God of Jacob. The God who pursued Jacob until he became the recipient of a beautiful blessing. The God of Erin. The God who formed me in my mother's womb. The God who moved mountains in my life by guiding me through difficulties. The God who has blessed me time and time again. The God who sees me. This God is your God too. Press into Him, trust Him, even when it is difficult, He will show up.

Chapter 7

Beauty For Ashes

LOVED BEYOND MEASURE

Loved. Beyond. Measure. As I have said, I am a civil engineering student, very into math, and just about every class I have has some type of measuring component. There are units for weight, pressure, force, density, gravity, speed, velocity, height, width, depth, but there are even more than just mathematical units. There are grades, job titles, addresses, and so much more. Think of a baby, at birth the first thing that happens is measurement, length and weight. Everything in this world is related to some type of measurement.

This has just now occurred to me. Realize that does not bring into effect monetary measurement, prices of materialistic possessions, or high-end education. To some extent it is a very human thing, to quantify everything and anything. Yet, at the same time, I think God intended it. He had a plan, and He created this universe which is wildly mathematically and scientifically based. Nevertheless, He, the Creator of this divine mathematical equation called our universe, stands outside of it all. His power knows no bounds, no amount of joules equates to His power. His knowledge has no bounds, even a man with every degree offered in the world would still not equate to His knowledge. Most importantly, His love knows no bounds. He loves beyond measure. It's incomprehensible. There are only two comparable aspects of life that come to mind for me. First was the ocean. The ocean freaks me out for the lack of knowledge we have about it, but at the same time, it has been very much so quantified. We know its bounds, besides its depths, it's very apparent where land ends and ocean starts. To some extent that is not even a plausible comparison. The second comparison is space, which I think could be a beautiful idea.

I also believe wholeheartedly that we are not intended to understand God fully. He is so far above us that our human minds cannot comprehend His vastness. For me, space seemingly just starts to put Him in perspective.

*Think about yourself, then think about the size of your town in comparison to the size of your state/territory. Now think of the size of your state/territory in comparison to the size of your country. Now think of your country in comparison to the size of the continent you live on. So forth and so on. Now think of the earth in comparison to the size of the sun. (1.3 **million** earths can fit in the sun) And to only think, our sun is just one of many stars like it, in a galaxy that is one of about two trillion. That's wild.*

Yet, He has this way of making everything okay, despite the reality that we are essentially microscopic on the universal scale. I just finished my fall semester in 2022, and I have to say this last week is one I will remember forever. Finals were stressful, again more so because I self-impose unrealistic expectations, but we are working on that. Yet, that was not what made this week memorable. Last weekend, I found out some disheartening news about not being able to go on a trip I had planned. I was so excited for this trip, and it is a month away. The initial impact of the idea that I could not go was hard. Then as it unfolded this week, I saw God work in miraculous ways.

First a quick backstory that will make this all the more understandable. As I mentioned, I went to Costa Rica in 2019, and fell in love with the people and the country. Ever since I stepped foot back in the States, I wanted to return to Costa Rica. I was fighting everything, including God trying to forge my way back. I struggled, I planned, and every single one of those plans failed. Now, after three and a half years I understand why, somewhat. About July, I do not remember the time or day, but I remember having this revelation that I have a winter break that is three and a half weeks long. I did know this, but I now realized that I could use that time to go back to you know where… Costa Rica. So there went my thoughts, and my heart. Yet, I had learned to not get too excited because of all the prior attempts that were my feudal chances at something God did not have for me in that season. Then I was just prayerfully considering for a bit and had a heart to ask my dad to go with me. I asked, and he said yes, but to some extent it was still a very up in the air hope. I knew my dad wanted to go, but the timing with work was incredibly unrealistic. By the time my dad decided he couldn't go, it was a month until the trip. So I sat, I prayed and talked to my mom, and ended up asking a friend, who said yes on the spot. It blew me away. Everything fell into place. I would be going to Costa Rica and then on the other trip I had planned. I was so excited.

Now back to this past week, the shoe dropped last weekend about the chances of me not being able to go on my second trip. I did something that I didn't realize how much I needed. I love to journal, so I went straight to the pages, and I was reading the Word, specifically Psalms. One theme I have noticed and admired about David is his heart of worship despite his highs and lows. So Holy Spirit whispered to me, Worship. As of late, the song Highs and Lows by Hillsong has been a favorite, little did I know why ("Highs & Lows Lyrics"). I put it on and poured out my heart. I was disappointed at the idea of not going, but more so, I wanted His Will to be done. I will admit, I have said that many times, but I truly meant it this time. I laid my brokenness, my lack of control, and my desires at His feet. I told Him that I trust Him (something I find myself struggling to do). Then I listened to the song I Surrender by Hillsong ... and this beautiful peace washed over me ("I Surrender"). I knew He would work, but I did not know how. Part of me was hoping I could still go. The next day I was told I couldn't.

I was sad, but I felt at peace. I don't really know how to explain it, but I felt like David. I was disappointed, but I held hopeful expectations knowing that God had a better plan in mind. That plan, go to Costa Rica for longer. At first, I was nervous to even bring this up because I didn't want to be forcing anything. Yet again, it fell into place before my eyes. My friend in Costa Rica could have us longer, my friend could go earlier, and the flight change was quite simple.

I am not saying this to gain any reverence or acknowledgement, I share this as an answer. An answer to the question I get so often, Why? (Also heard in forms of Why give your life to someone you can't see? Why not just do what you want and get saved on your last day? Why do you want to follow all those rules?) This story right here is why. Because I serve a God who cares, and who loves me so much. He knew I would make it back to Costa Rica, but on His terms solely because it is so much better than anything I could've forced. He loves me so incredibly much that the only thing I want to do is serve Him. In short, my answer is typically "Because He has walked with me through my worst days and best and loved me through both". This is so beautiful, this is what people desire in a relationship, and He does it perfectly.

This is the gift I desire to show to the world. I would love to give you three steps to know you are loved by God, but it isn't that simple. Point blank period, He loves you, that isn't the issue. The issue is us, we are broken, and have been hurt by others. Those scars from relationships with other humans bar our relationship with God. This is why there is no formula to not only knowing He loves you but feeling His love in your heart. He has every intention to be in a relationship with you. His love isn't too far or too good to be true. My struggle is trust, and even with what I feel was a monumental moment in my relationship with Him, I still need to work on trusting Him.

All of this is what God desires for our life. He desires to bring beauty from ashes in all areas of our life, small and big. He desires to redeem the parts of ourselves we can hardly bear. He craves redemption for our failures and mistakes. This does not go to say that we will not have to deal with the consequences of our mistakes, but it does go to say that God can bring beauty from every and any situation.

That being said, wherever you are at, keep going. You never know when your next aha moment with Him will be. One thing I can promise you is the more you press into Him, the more He will show up. The more your giants seem to shrink, because you start to see them through His eyes. You will start to see that there is no length that He won't go for you. It won't be easy, but it will be worth every smile and every tear. He will help you, keep going.

COMPARISON

What a topic. Comparison can be a good thing... said no one ever, but I believe it. There is comparison in every single aspect of life, just like measurement. If you're like me, you compare the night of sleep you had to the ones prior every morning. Or you compare your cup of coffee to the one you got at Starbucks last week. Or you compare your first task you did at your job to what you do now. Or you compare turkey to ham depending on what you feel like having for lunch. Simplified, yes, but comparison isn't always a bad thing. Comparison is what shows us there is more. Comparison is a gift from God that illuminates how much more in store He could have for you.

In a discussion about good and evil, someone once asked me, "If God is good then why did He even let sin and bad things happen?". I was surprised by the depth of the question; I have thought about this before and was trying to align my thoughts. Then another person answered something along the lines of "Because if there wasn't brokenness and evil, we wouldn't recognize the goodness of God as goodness". Wow that hit me like a Mack truck. I personally always thought about free will when this topic came up. I think that God allowed sin and evil into the world because He gave us free will. Yet this other perspective was raw, real, and challenging. This is where the idea of comparison being good can be found. Just like the highs and lows of life, you wouldn't recognize the highs if it weren't for the lows. You wouldn't feel the liberation at the end of a semester, if you didn't go to school. You wouldn't recognize a friend as a close reliable person until they had walked through hardship with you and proven they were close and reliable.

This illuminates a new way to look at comparison. Nonetheless, the more popular view on comparison is one of a derogatory connotation. It is one that brings feelings of inadequacy, jealousy, pride, and heartache.

I struggled with this in my younger years. As a kid, I already mentioned how I hated who I was as a person to some extent. I disliked the thought of being someone I was not. Then I was freed from that thanks to Jesus. I was given a new opportunity to be the person I truly believed I was. Yet, alongside this opportunity came the feeling of having to prove myself, but not in the ways I used to. When it came to academics, I was in good classes and did well, and for sports I enjoyed them, but I was far from a superstar. Despite what you might expect, I was really happy with this. Yet, a door opened that I didn't expect.

As a young girl, you are always subjected to comments about your body. It is kind of wild how normalized it is to comment on a young girl's body. Despite the context - from 'you are so skinny, do you eat?' to 'maybe you should lose a few pounds'. It is sad how we let this fly as a society. I am not going to preach body positivity from a soap box. Yet, I needed it. Jesus saw my broken heart. He saw the disappointment in my eyes when I looked in a mirror. He knew my heart's desire to fit the mold. Yet, He also saw my beauty all along. He knew that it would only take time for me to recognize it too. He knew that in time, there would be a day that I would look in the mirror and smile.

I don't share this out of pride, I still struggle here and there with body image, but I do fully believe that God walked me through it in order to give me the ability to walk with others through it. I was neck deep in the comparison hole. Let me tell you, if you are conscious about your body, I would not recommend being on the track team. I was constantly comparing myself to girls who were next to no body fat. I was so aware of my size it was sickening. I don't wish it on anyone, but I know a lot of girls go through it. I know that it is only going to get worse with how social media is reaching younger and younger people.

The way God got me out? It was one step that had to be repeated many times, and pursued, and fought for. First, let me tell you how it came to be.

I am a lover of sunsets. I love all nature, but there is something about the sky. That means that I often go down to the river and watch the sunset. I love it, I always have been enamored by the quietness of a sunset spent with Jesus. Whether that means just worship or reading or drawing, it is bliss for me. That being said, I was sitting one night at my favorite place, and I thought "Wow God, you've outdone yourself once again, your masterpieces are simply stunning". Then came the blow to the jaw. He whispered to my heart, 'You say you love my sunsets and creation, but you hate your body which is just as much my creation as the sunset'. I was humbled to say the least. I knew I needed to learn to not hate my body, but I didn't know how.

This is where the one step comes in. The step? Controlling your tongue. I was the biggest issue. I was the one tearing myself down over thick thighs and monkey toes. I was the one who repetitively tore myself down. Then I realized, if I ever spoke to someone the way I spoke to myself, I would expect to get punched. So that is the step, stop talking to yourself as if you're meaningless. You are loved, you are beautiful, you are a masterpiece of the Most High.

He has so much in store for you. Let me tell you, looking back and comparing how I lived when I was ashamed of my body to how I live now, I know that there is so much freedom in seeing yourself through God's eyes. He will show you how He sees you and He sees you as more precious than gold. He will always prove to you how much you are loved, so let Him. Stop talking to a Daughter of the King like she is worthless.

YOU ARE CHOSEN

There is a beauty in knowing who you are in Christ. There is an assurance and peace that it brings. I truly believe this assurance and peace is impossible to find anywhere else.

The sad fact is that the world is searching for exactly this. To be chosen, to be loved, to be known. There is a desire for these things that people feel, but do not realize what it is. There is an urgency to fill this void. Yet, an inability to acknowledge the root of the feelings.

The irreplaceable joy in the matter is that there is something that will fill the void. There is an answer. On the verge of being too forward, the answer is Jesus. Jesus is the One who came to earth, for you specifically, and made the decision that you were worth the cross.

You were worth the excruciating pain and agony that He endured. The even more beautifully humbling fact is that if you were the only person on the planet to be saved, He still would have done it. He loves you so infinitely much that He chose you. He chose you to live the life you lead. He chose you to be redeemed, forgiven, and set free. He chose you to step into the love He has for you.

So why do we not live like these things are true? Why do we recognize them but not resonate with them?

Why don't we live like these are true? Two common reasons I have encountered are either a person doesn't know the truth, or a person sees Christianity with a tainted perspective. The second is a large part of why I wrote this book in the first place. Nonetheless, let's start with the first. This is explicitly outlined in Romans 10.

Romans 10:14

How, then, can they call on the one they have not believed in? And how can they believe in the one of whom they have not heard? And how can they hear without someone preaching to them?

This comes to show that it is almost an obvious result for someone not to believe if they haven't heard. This comes into play with us being chosen in two ways. One, we are chosen to have received the gift that God so graciously sent, His Son. Two, you are chosen to share that gift. The next chapter goes more in depth into our responsibilities to reach the lost, but it still holds value in the sense that God not only chose you to be a part of His family, but He also chose you and invites you into His plan. This is so cool to me as we are not a dire component. In fact, we aren't necessary at all. If God wanted redemption for every soul on the planet, He could do it.

Yet, He invites us into His cause, a cause of togetherness with the very One who created us. How beautiful.

Now back to the second reason I often encounter when I have spoken to people about Christ: a tainted view of Christianity. How or why? Well pick any of the aforementioned topics, like church people, legalism, and judgment. This is a sad reality that I have come to notice is a wedge between the lost becoming whole in Christ. Again, nothing that God cannot redeem or restore, but I still believe that there is work to be done on account of this reality. Love is the solution above all things. I believe the more we seek to reflect the unconditional love that God has for us, the more we will start counteracting the poor stereotype that is entangled with today's Christians. A close second is humility. Humility to recognize the need for a Savior, humility to see ourselves as exactly equal with those around us, and humility to be going where others won't for the sake of the Gospel. Each and every one of us is chosen on an intimate level, yet we cannot mistake the idea of being chosen with the idea of being better than others.

Now why do we recognize that we are redeemed, forgiven, and set free, but do not resonate with it.

That is hard. In all honesty, I think it comes in waves. At least for me it does. I know God's love. I knew God's love when I first got saved, but it resonates in my heart more now than ever, and I know that the longer I live the more it will resonate. I don't know if there is a cookie cutter answer for why we don't all resonate with the reality of what God has to offer in the same way or on a timeline, but that right there may just be the beauty of it. It comes to show that our

God is personal. He wants us to know and feel the redemption and freedom, but we are all unique and so will our experiences be.

THERE IS MORE

It is easy to get wrapped up in the more. Especially in Western culture, more is always expected. You can climb the corporate ladder, and "get to the top". Then realize that it isn't enough, so you find a hobby, sports cars. Buy a few, only to discover another brand you like and buy a few more. Then your house needs a bigger garage, so a bigger house it is too. When does it stop? The reality of it is, it doesn't. There is no amount of material things that will ever be enough. Yet, many spend their days attempting to attain the unattainable.

On the other hand, there is always spiritual gain to be had. There is more hope, more faith, more trust that can be attained. There is more of anything that falls on our side of the interaction between us and God. Meaning, we can have more faith, love, and hope. God cannot. God's faith, love, and hope cannot grow. He is as faithful as He was when He delivered the Israelites from Egypt and as faithful as He ever will be. He loves us just the same from our first breath to our last no matter what happens in between. He hopes for our future and our tomorrows just as much as He did when He formed us in our mother's womb. So where is there more to be had? There is more to be had simply for more people. We can share what we have with more people. We can grow by exercising our faith and trust in God. We can know the Scriptures more, we can pray more, we can love more.

The beauty in this is that a destination is just as unattainable as it is for materialistic gain. Nonetheless, these practices bid us to be better, and more Christ-like. They grant us a closer relationship with the Father, and continued evidence of His character throughout. A life chasing Jesus is a life, not free of worry or pain, but one that is a continuous journey with more always in the forefront.

God will never stop working. It is simply time we get on board with that idea. There is no number of people that will satisfy the Lord's desire to make His name known, and to be a part of His creation's lives. There is no distance traveled that will satisfy the Lord's heart. So as life with Christ may be difficult, it is fulfilling, and there will always be more to be done.

The question is what are we willing to spend our lives doing? Chasing what is freeing or chasing what is fleeting?

WHAT CAN WE DO

It is easier said than done, but we can start living in the reality of who God made us to be. Our God is One who redeems and brings beauty from ashes. It may be body dysmorphia, it may be sin issues that have left you in what seems to be an inescapable hole, or it may be something that was inflicted on you; no matter the circumstance, He can and will deliver you from it and bring beauty from ashes. We can ask for help with that, from both the One who made us and our community around us. I know it isn't easy, and honestly it can be very uncomfortable, but God loves us and chose us to be set apart. He wants us to resonate deeply with the forgiveness and love He has offered us. He wants us to walk into more with Him.

Even more so, the more we press into Him and what He has for us, the better we will be at reflecting it. If you were unaware of who an actor was, could you impersonate them well? Probably not. The same goes for God, not that we should be impersonating God or Christ, but how do you intend to model your life after someone if you don't know them deeply?

Christ was deeply known and deeply knew the Father, their relationship sustained Christ while on earth. I would beg to argue that our Christian walks would look radically different if we were sustained first and foremost by our walk with God.

CHAPTER 8

WHAT CAN WE DO

GOING FORTH

Christ calls us to not just come to Him, but to come to Him and to in turn go and tell others. What does that actually look like? Moving to Africa, Cambodia, or some other part of the world? Not necessarily. Christ calls us to go to all areas. He calls us to go to the area we are in, then the areas surrounding that, and then the uttermost parts of the world. He calls the kingdom to be kingdom minded. If everyone were to go, who would reach the lost that are our neighbors. If everyone were to stay, who would reach those who have yet to hear the name of Jesus. Going forth can look different for everybody.

I have spent some time overseas. As well as doing missionary work domestically. I love overseas work and truly see myself doing that long term. The first time I went to Mexico I was enamored. I fell in love with reaching and serving people. The second time was when I knew that this had to be my lifestyle in the future, that this is what God made me to do. Yet, my third overseas trip challenged me in a way I would hope for others to understand without having to go overseas three times. That is the fact that people on your block need Jesus just as much as the people in remote villages in Costa Rica. At the time, God really challenged me with the idea: if you want to be a missionary make it your lifestyle now. Reach your high school, and later your university. Reach those who are closest to you. They need me. That was difficult. Yet, God has not ceased to amaze me. He has made opportunities arise and conversations happen with the people I would least expect.

All that being said, I encourage you to go forth. I encourage you to pray for conversations. Just know God will answer that prayer so be willing and able to have conversations about Him even in situations that may make you nervous.

I Peter 3:15-16

But in your hearts set apart Christ as Lord. Always be prepared to give an answer to everyone who asks you to give the reason for the hope that you have. But do this with gentleness and respect, keeping a clear conscience, so that those who speak maliciously against your good behavior in Christ may be ashamed of their slander.

Story time, I had recently gone away to a discipleship program where I met an amazing group of people. Since then, we have been trying to stay in touch by doing weekly calls. One week, a friend of mine asked how I can be praying for you? I paused and said, "I don't want to give you a blanket request, like strength or peace, so give me a second". After thinking I said, "I would like to pray for opportunities to reach my coworkers". There and then we prayed over the phone for the hearts of my coworkers. For some insight, I work at an engineering firm, not overly professional to the point that we aren't friendly, but it isn't the place I would quickly bring up my faith. The very next day after that call, I ended up being in my coworker's office for over an hour talking about my faith, and his beliefs on the matter.

Not saying that the turnaround time will always be 24 hours, but God wants people to know His heart for them, so praying for conversations is praying into His will. This is something that will give you space to go forth, and help you start to recognize through the power of the Holy Spirit when these opportunities arise.

There is a beauty in seeing the world through the lens of the Holy Spirit. A beauty that can be utterly terrifying.

I think that the reality of the situation is that it is hard to get prayer integrated into your life to the point that it is a habit. Then comes the harsh reality that prayer works. Praying for people is going to open doors for you to talk to people, to share the Word with people, and to have a front row to see God change lives. All amazingly daunting tasks.

Psalm 111:3

Glorious and majestic are his deeds, and his righteousness endures
forever.

I guess my two cents would be to get comfortable with being uncomfortable. I think that no matter how well versed you are in Scripture it is going to be difficult to talk to someone. It is never going to feel 100% comfortable. There are going to be times that it does not happen as you expect. Yet, God can and will use a willing heart. No matter how ill equipped you feel or honestly you are, God can still use you. It is beautiful. I am so truthfully not equipped to do what God asks me to do on a daily basis. In all honesty, I never feel more ill equipped than in the moment. However, time and time again God shows up and He works, and His majestic works are put on display once again. That is the beauty, that we aren't meant to be comfortable because it isn't in our own strength, it is all His. It is the work of the Holy Spirit, the breath of the Almighty that moves mountains, we simply have the privilege to witness it, and take part in it.

Job 32: 7-9

I thought, 'Age should speak;

advanced years should teach wisdom.'

But it is the spirit in a man,

the breath of the Almighty, that gives him understanding.

It is not only the old who are wise,

not only the aged who understand what is right.

REVITALIZING YOUR DAY TO DAY

Habits is a topic as of late that I could go on for hours about. Habits are so wildly interesting considering how mundane they are as well as how life altering they are. So what does it look like to revitalize your life?

First off, I would have to write another book, but one has been written that is so amazing and I could not write anything even close. If you are truly serious about changing your habits, go read The Common Rule by Justin Earley (*The Common Rule).*

There is a power unlike any other that is creating a habit. A singular habit can change your life. Dramatic? Sounds like it, but I have seen it become a reality in both good and bad ways. The idea of breaking a habit is widely acknowledged as difficult, because it is. I propose something different, replacing habits. This is where real life change can be attained. Habitually, before I went to bed, I used to scroll. Most times, I would set a timer, and end up ignoring that timer when it went off. This was an unhealthy habit, one I really tried to break but couldn't. It wasn't until I decided I would set a timer to pray each night instead. I set a timer not to limit my prayer, but to keep myself accountable from falling asleep. This has stuck. Simply enough, breaking a habit is horrifically difficult, replacing it on the other hand is not as daunting.

The reality of our world today is that we are a technology driven society in the west. We are quick to check our phones and in turn we have become an anxious group of people. When you sit and truly think about the choke hold our technology has on us, it is not that surprising that anxiety rates have risen just as much as cell phone sales. The vibration or ringtone of a phone sends your mind straight into action. Who is it? What do they need? Is it someone I feel like talking to? Is it an emergency? Is it a work call? Is it an interview I have been waiting for? Is it a family member? These are very few of the questions our mind runs through just in the mere moments from acknowledging the vibration or ringtone. Then the assessment comes, and you answer all of those questions, answers that may put your mind at ease or cause an addition to a never ending mental to do list.

I am not against technology. I think that technology is a resourceful tool that we can use. Yet, like most things there is a sense of duality that begs that just as much good that can be achieved, so can bad. The mental readiness that we are constantly supporting in order to be able to be ready to be reached at all times is draining. There is no need for one singular person to be accessed twenty-four hours a day, seven days a week. Yet, we don't live in that reality. We live in the reality that our phone is an extension of ourselves. It isn't. You are whole without your devices. You are capable of surviving without them. The question is if we are willing to be. Are we willing to come to terms with the fact that we aren't needed every second of every day? That can be the root of attachment to a device. The need to be needed. Are we willing to step into the countercultural idea of silence, of sitting with self. I truly believe that our phones occupy so much of our minds that we have lost touch with ourselves to the point that we do not understand ourselves. Maybe if we spent more time alone, in true solitude, we would become more familiar with ourselves. We would understand what makes us tick, and what ticks us off. What if rather than taking a mental break on social media, taking a true mental break and checking in with our emotions. Recognizing why we are feeling the way we are feeling, and starting to understand how to counteract the negative emotions we feel but so often suppress. This would lead to a self-awareness that would simply bid a healthier mindset.

This would also free our time to be invested in others. We have all been there, overly excited to share something when the listener is engulfed in a screen with your life story as background noise. It is sad, it is real though. I have experienced it, and I have done it. This charges us to go forth. This makes us better at listening. This begs for our stamina to be able to build better habits. To break the chains of the habits we don't even recognize. Habits that are slowly molding our lives as we subconsciously perform them over and over again.

Again, with the two cents, start small. Change nighttime scrolling to a few minutes of prayer, but do not pick the phone back up afterward. From there build up, add spiritual disciplines in place of monotonous habits. Rather than watching the news every morning, get in the Word or listen to a podcast. These are small things that carry way more influence than we give them credit for. It all starts somewhere, and it is worth every effort, I can promise you that.

SOWING INTO RELATIONSHIPS

Where to begin. This topic has rattled my life over the past year and a half. It has changed my perspective, it has changed the way I interact with others, and with God. It has changed my view of God, and it has radically revived my soul.

Let's begin with how it has changed my view of God. There are some areas of life that I am very quick to shy away from. I am not one for a party / bar scene, never have been, and never will be. I truly struggle with how I believe people should interact with alcohol. I am not here to get political or fight over what the Bible means when it talks about wine. I am here with a genuine heart, trying to show how God revealed Himself to me. Over the last six months, I turned 21 and in the United States it means that drinking is legal. I have since been invited out on many different occasions to different scenes. I internally struggled with this a lot when it first happened. I was so sure that any place where alcohol was, was not for me. I found myself so in my head, but to some degree recognized that I was sacrificing relationships with my peers for my preconceived notions. While in college I truly believe that my main purpose is to be a light to those around me. To reach the people next to me. But how? How am I supposed to reach people if I am so worried about me, that I love them from a distance. This is where the idea of genuine relational living shook my life and my view of God. I was invited out and I prayed over it, and I decided to go. It is also important to note that I do not have any previous history of drinking, and do not get tempted in the slightest to drink when in social situations, or at all for that matter. So I went. There was drinking involved, but overall it was mostly just a bunch of my peers hanging out on a Friday night. There were no extremes and I enjoyed getting to see my new friends outside of the classroom setting. The next day I felt dirty, I felt that I had messed up and was guilty of being a two-faced Christian.

I sat and I cried. I had done what so many adults had told me to avoid. What you always hear growing up: Don't go to parties, Don't be with the wrong crowd, Be careful of what others perceive. While there is some truth in these statements, they are also not entirely full proof. The point-blank reality of the night prior was that I went to a friend's house with the intention of building relationships with my peers for the sake of them seeing Jesus in me. That is what happened. Yet, I felt like a complete and utter failure. This is when I turned to the Word. I opened my Bible, tears rolling, and asked God why He had given me peace if I felt like this. I turned to Matthew and read the story of Jesus eating with the tax collectors. A story best if read, not explained.

Matthew 9 :10-13

While Jesus was having dinner at Matthew's house, many tax collectors and "sinners" came and ate with him and his disciples. When the Pharisees saw this, they asked his disciples, "Why does your teacher eat with tax collectors and 'sinners'?"

On hearing this, Jesus said, "It is not the healthy who need a doctor, but the sick. But go and learn what this means: 'I desire mercy, not sacrifice.' For I have not come to call the righteous, but sinners."

This shattered my view of God in the best way possible. Jesus, the perfect man, God incarnate, was found sitting with sinners. In all seriousness, that is what we all are. I realized that I was barring myself from being Christ-like by trying to tell people about Jesus without actually stepping into their lives. This was, as you can assume, highly ineffective. The other beautiful thing is that the religious people are the ones calling Jesus out. I was so concerned whether people would assume that I was partying when that wasn't the case. Yet, the fact of the matter is those who truly know me, know my intentions. Those who didn't know me met me in the same sober mind they would have in the hallway between classes. Those who weren't there and made assumptions are comparable to the religious leaders in this story. This is when I came to the reality that I would rather be in Jesus' shoes in this story. This completely changed how I interact with believers and nonbelievers. I would rather be judged for something innocent than judge for someone taking up their cross and reaching the lost. Now this comes with a disclaimer, I would not encourage every person to go to bars to tell people about Jesus. If you have a past with a temptation or struggle, I am not encouraging putting yourself in a situation that could lead to you falling back into sin. I am suggesting that we as Christians lose the tendency to disassociate when we feel that our own reputations may be at risk.

Proverbs 29:25

Fear of man will prove to be a snare,

but whoever trusts in the Lord is kept safe.

Jesus' reputation preceded Him and ours should too. I can say that character is not solely defined by what you do on a Friday night. However, I can say that from my hesitant obedience to step into a more real relationship with those around me, God has moved. I have a huge expectation for Him to continue to do so.

The sad fact is that a lot of us Christians are so caught up in our own reputation that we aren't willing to love people how Jesus loved. We aren't willing to put the time in to learn how to be in the world, but not of it. That is where we need work. We need to learn to love as Jesus did. To sow into one-on-one relationships and to pursue true life change in others.

KINGDOM MINDED

Kingdom minded. A mind set on global unification. I know a hefty phrase. A phrase I heard prior to my first trip to Costa Rica that has stuck with me ever since. What does that even mean? Well, I think one of the most awe-inspiring attributes of the Father is that He has every single human on His mind at all times. He desires so deeply to have a relationship with each and every person. That is wonderful, but because of our fallen state it is far from reality. The current state of the world does not change God's heart for the nations. God still desires to know all of us even if we don't desire to know Him. Or if we don't know His name. Yes, there are many languages that do not contain a Bible, there are languages and tongues that do not have a word for God. That is why kingdom mindedness needs to be the focus. We are not simply living to live. We are living for Him.

Over time I have realized my desires have started to align with His. I have also been asked often why I even bother. Why help when there is always going to be more need? The truth is because when you get a gift that is so precious you long to share it. You long for others to be told about this gift. You long for others to recognize its beauty and worth. You long for others to understand why you esteem it so highly. It is simply the same with Jesus. I long for others to know the depths of His love, the value of His sacrifice, and the riches of His heart for us. I help because He did. He went for the one. He will always go for the one and that is all that matters to me anymore. Go for the one. Help bring one into the kingdom. Then another and another. Help others see the beauty of this gift we have been so freely given, this life that is meant to be lived to the full, and this heart of a Creator that longs for His creation to know Him.

Chasing Him is the only life worth living. Bringing the kingdom to earth while we can is the greatest privilege and biggest blessing. God wants us to enjoy our lives, He wants us to be free, and He desires for us to share this with others.

He desires more than anything for you to know Him deeply. No matter if you don't walk with Christ, you have been for eighty years, or anything in between. He desires to reveal more of Himself to you. Let Him in, and don't look back.

Epilogue

What a journey. All I can say is God is faithful. He truly will see you through. I am not going to lie; I am nervous to put this out there. There were multiple moments in writing this book where I just bawled my eyes out while filling the pages. It is more information than I tell most people about myself. But God. But God will do with it what He pleases, and if it can bring more glory to Him then so be it.

I want to thank you for reading my story. I often have thought that my story isn't powerful enough to share, but the Lord has slowly broken down those lies that I tell myself. So if you are out there and don't find yourself having a story like others in whatever way, still tell it. Tell it until you learn to love it because God wrote it just for you.

Every story matters and He loves you *More Than Lilies.*

NOTES

Chapter 4

1. "Inadequate." Merriam-Webster.com Dictionary, Merriam-Webster, https://www.merriam-webster.com/dictionary/inadequate. Accessed 16 Jan. 2024.

2. "I Surrender" Words and Music by Matt Crocker © 2011 Hillsong Music Publishing (APRA) CCLI: 6177317

3. "Highs & Lows Lyrics." Lyrics.com. STANDS4 LLC, 2024. Web. 16 Jan. 2024. <https://www.lyrics.com/lyric/35222203/Hillsong+Young+%26+Free/Highs+%26+Lows>.

Chapter 6

1. Dreikurs, Rudolph. 1964.

2. Collins, Jim. *Good to Great*. Studentsonly®, 2009.

Chapter 7

1. "Jireh" Written by Chandler Moore, Chris Brown, Steven Furtick, & Naomi Raine © 2021 Elevation Worship Records.

Chapter 8

1. Earley, Justin Whitmel. *The Common Rule: Habits of Purpose for an Age of Distraction*. IVP, an Imprint of InterVarsity Press, 2023.